B. Charlotte Stephenson

308 Whitman Court
Buchanan, MI 49107

HOLY SONGS OF ISRAEL

Inspirational Worship from the Psalms

RABBI YECHIEL ECKSTEIN

HOLY SONGS OF ISRAEL

Inspirational Worship from the Psalms

RABBI YECHIEL ECKSTEIN

 International Fellowship of Christians and Jews®

Holy Songs of Israel:
Inspirational Worship from the Psalms

Cover and interior design by **Design Corps**,
Batavia, IL and Colorado Springs, CO
(www.designcorps.us)
Project staff: Art Cooley, Moshe Rothchild, Denise
Jones, John LaRue, Betsy Schmitt, Katie Windisch

Published by the *International Fellowship of
Christians and Jews* with offices in Australia, Canada,
Israel, South Korea, and the United States.

ISBN 978-0-9835327-2-9

First printing: 2013

IMAGES CREDITS

Cover:
Wheat Field at Sunset (photography by Benji
Cooper) and *Musical Notes on a Curled Page*
from **Getty Images**

*Rome King David from the Maria Column by
Spain Statis* from **Shutterstock**

*Rabbi Yechiel Eckstein with Guitar at New
Life Church* from **IFCJ**

Psalm Twenty Three from **iStockphoto**.

Interior:
All images are from **iStockphoto**
except for the following:
Shutterstock — pp. vi, and 57
IFCJ — pg. 71
Israeli Government Press Office — pg. 96
Flash90 — pg. 100
Getty Images — pp. 44, and 111

TABLE OF CONTENTS

HOLY SONGS OF PRAISE TO GOD

"Come, let us sing for joy to the LORD." — PSALMS 95:1

With these words, King David invites us to join him in reciting the psalms, or as they are known in Hebrew, *Tehillim*. The word *Tehillim* comes from a word meaning "to praise," but the psalms are far more than acknowledging God's goodness. They are the very vehicle through which centuries of Jews and Christians have risen above life's challenges in order to remember and encounter their Creator.

The book of Psalms is one of the greatest gifts ever given to humankind. As the renowned 19th century Rabbi Menachem Mendel Schneerson said, "If one would only know the power of the verses of Psalms, and their effect on high, one would never stop saying them. The verses of Psalms transcend all barriers and ascend higher and higher, imploring the Master of the Universe until they achieve results in kindness and mercy." Through this beloved book, King David hands us the keys that unlock the gates of heaven.

But what exactly are the psalms? For many, they are deep and meaningful prayers archived and compiled into one book. Yet, they also assume a prominent place in Scripture, the very Word of God. So are they our message to God, or His message to us? The answer is both, which is why the psalms are so very powerful. As we immerse ourselves in this ancient poetry, we are talking to God and hearing Him speak at the same time. The verses form a portal that connects us directly to the throne of the Almighty.

In the pages that follow you will find a selection of psalms that are prominent in the Jewish tradition today. For each psalm, you will discover who wrote the psalm and why. Together, we will examine the psalm and understand how it is used in Jewish worship then and now. In addition, through devotional reflection, we will learn how to apply the lessons found in each psalm to our lives in a meaningful and inspirational way.

When David gave us the book of Psalms, he bequeathed a great gift to all humanity throughout the ages. It is my hope that this book will help you unwrap that gift and reveal the depth and magnitude of this stunning legacy for all peoples of faith.

Rabbi Eckstein

Introducing the Holy Songs of Israel

The book of Psalms is generally attributed to King David. Yet many of the individual psalms are attributed to other authors that include Adam, Abraham, Moses, the three sons of Korah, Solomon, and several others. So why is David given credit for the entire work? Because it was David who compiled them and established them as a form of worship. And it was David, *"the hero of Israel's songs"* (2 Samuel 23:1), who instituted the practice of worship with soul-stirring music and inspirational songs.

Each psalm was meant to be accompanied by music, and indeed, many of them begin with musical instruction, as in Psalm 4:1, *"For the director of music. With stringed instruments. A psalm of David."* The psalms were intended for use in the Temple that David's son Solomon would eventually build. David understood that feelings and emotions were a key component in the worship of God. In fact, Jewish tradition teaches that God Himself said to David, "One day of your songs and praises is more precious to Me than the thousands of offerings that will be brought by your son Solomon." God has always preferred our hearts above all else. The music of the priests together with David's psalms would send hearts soaring all the way to God.

Even without the music, which was lost in the years of exile that followed the destruction of the Temple, David's psalms are brimming with passion and inspiration. They give voice to every facet of human emotion – from the depths of despair, worry, regret, and pain, to the heights of triumph, hope, joy, and ecstasy. For every life experience, there is a psalm. And it's no wonder. King David's life ran the gamut of emotions. He himself experienced just about every type of situation, and with all that he went through, there was a song – a psalm – on his lips. David wrote, *"Every day I will praise You and extol Your name forever and ever"* (Psalm 145:2).

Today, the psalms are at the core of every faith-centered life. For both Jews and Christians, the book of Psalms plays an integral part in formal communal worship. In Judaism, psalms are part of the daily service, and additional psalms are recited on Festivals and the New Moon, each psalm reflecting that particular occasion.

Outside our synagogues and churches, the psalms are just as central to our relationship with God. In times of great joy and also in moments of extreme distress, King David's psalms are the harp upon which we express our emotions to God. There are psalms designated for times of illness, danger, and war. There are psalms composed for moments of thanksgiving, forgiveness, and protection. And because the power of the psalms is said to be so great, some folks make it a point to complete the entire book of Psalms every month, or every week, or even every day. Several millennia after it was written, this ancient manuscript remains very much a part of our lives today.

King David ends the book of Psalms with these words: "*Let everything that has breath praise the LORD*" (Psalms 150:6). The final message of the psalms is that every living creature should sing, and will eventually learn to sing, the praises of the Lord. The Sages teach that there is another way to understand this verse. Instead of reading the verse "*everything that has breath praise the LORD,*" they teach us to read the verse, "praise the Lord for every breath." Not only should everything learn to praise the Lord, we should also learn to praise the Lord for *everything*. The good, the bad, our depths and our heights, our joy and our sorrow – it's all a beautiful symphony whose many different tones and movements create the magnum opus that is our lives.

PSALM 1

FOR THE LORD
WATCHES OVER
THE PATH OF
THE GODLY, BUT
THE PATH OF THE
WICKED LEADS TO
DESTRUCTION.

—PSALM 1:6

A SONG OF GUIDANCE

Psalm 1 opens the door to the book of Psalms. As the psalm chosen to begin King David's epic work, it answers some important questions: For whom were the psalms written and for what purpose? Rabbi Yudan, a 4th century scholar living in Israel, called this psalm "the choicest of all Psalms." It is a prime example of

David's poetry and gets to the heart of what the book of Psalms is all about.

So, who is King David's target audience? The answer is found in the first few words of the psalm. In English, the text reads: *"Blessed is the one…"* (v. 1). But a more literal translation of the original Hebrew reads: *"Blessed is the man . . ."* To whom is the psalmist speaking? Everyone. All of us. Not scholars, not royalty, and not the already righteous. The psalms were written for the average person experiencing the journey of life. It's a guidebook for everyone.

The first psalm cuts right to the chase. As a guidebook for life, Psalm 1 lays out the map and shows us the path. Don't go here: *"Blessed is the one who does not walk in step with the wicked . . ."* (v. 1). Do this instead: *"Blessed is the one . . . who meditates on his law day and night"* (vv. 1–2). And if we stay away from bad and stick to God's path, we will prosper (v. 3). The wicked, on the other hand, walk a path that leads them to destruction. Psalm 1 gives us a basic overview of the terrain of life and shows us the most direct route to our desired destination.

The rest of the psalms cover the many stops that we will make along life's journey. Whether on a rocky climb or a smooth downhill, King David has a psalm for every occasion. There are many different kinds of psalms—those of thanks, those of prayer, those of praise, and many more. Some are written from a place of joy and others from deep sorrow. But all of the psalms have one thing in common—David's psalms give us perspective and keep us moving in the right direction.

It is customary to read Psalm 1 at funerals. In fact, this psalm begins a Jewish funeral. As the guests are seated quietly and the casket is brought in, the reader begins the recitation of Psalm 1. It is both a eulogy for the deceased and a message for the living. We honor the life that was by praising the deceased for walking on the godly path. But this psalm is also a jarring wake-up call for those still on their journey. It encourages us to re-evaluate the direction that we have chosen and guides us toward the path that we should be taking. This psalm is a sober reminder of the need to stay focused on our ultimate goal—to stay on the path of the godly.

A CHRISTIAN SONG

When Peace Like a River
BASED ON PSALM 1:3

When peace like a river
attendeth my way,

when sorrows like
sea billows roll;

whatever my lot,
thou hast taught
me to say,

"It is well, it is well
with my soul."

Refrain:

It is well with my soul;

it is well, it is well
with my soul.

—Horatio Gates Spafford
(1828–1888)

Psalm 1

BLESSED IS THE
ONE WHO DOES
NOT WALK IN STEP
WITH THE WICKED
OR STAND IN THE
WAY THAT SINNERS
TAKE OR SIT IN
THE COMPANY OF
MOCKERS, BUT
WHOSE DELIGHT
IS IN THE LAW
OF THE LORD, AND
WHO MEDITATES
ON HIS LAW DAY
AND NIGHT.

—PSALM 1:1–2

The Path of Righteousness

 few years ago, I saw a short video clip about the nature of man. Dennis Prager, author and media personality, approaches random people on the street and asks them the following question: "Are you a good person?" Just about everyone answers, "Yes!" Then comes the follow-up question: "Why?"

Dennis presses them, "What makes you good?" The answers are all different. "I don't cheat on my taxes." "I don't kill anyone." "I don't steal." And so on. Interestingly, Dennis demonstrates that most people define their goodness by what that they *don't* do and not by what that they *do*.

So, the question for us: Is that enough? Can one be considered good by avoiding evil?

The psalmist echoes the voice of the common man when he lists the things a person should not do in order to be blessed: Don't walk with the wicked; don't stand with the sinners; and don't sit with the mockers. He mentions walking, standing, and sitting—the three things people do while they are active—as if to say, "don't do anything that bad people do."

The next logical step would be to tell us what we should be doing, but that line never comes. The closest we get is encouragement to delight in God's law and to meditate on it. While this is certainly praiseworthy, it's not exactly the action plan that we would expect.

Many people feel that righteousness is unattainable. But the book of Psalms begins by teaching us that it is totally within reach. We only need to

DEVOTION

stop ourselves from doing evil and we will have made our Creator very happy.

Really? Can that possibly be enough?

The psalm begins: *"Blessed is the 'ish'. . ."* *Ish* is the Hebrew word for man. God expects us to be human, not saints. Just be human, says God, and the rest will follow. By the end of the psalm, the 'man' is called righteous because a person who refrains from evil will naturally engage in goodness.

Oskar Schindler, made famous by the movie *Schindler's List,* saved almost 1,200 Jewish lives during the Holocaust. Schindler was no saint. At the beginning, he was just a guy out to make a buck when he hired over 1,000 Jewish workers to work in his factory. But with time, Schindler started to protect his workers and save their lives. Schindler never considered himself a hero, and neither did those who knew him well. Schindler was quoted as saying, "I knew the people who worked for me. . . . When you know people, you have to behave toward them like human beings." Just by acting like a human being, Schindler became a hero and earned himself a place among the "Righteous Gentiles" for all eternity.

On the quest toward righteousness, start small. Can you speak less gossip? Can you count to ten when you get angry? Imagine what the world would look like if everyone took one step toward doing less evil, and therefore, doing more good.

GOING DEEPER FOR CHRISTIANS

For a Christian perspective on doing good, read:

- Matthew 5:16
- Romans 7:4
- Galatians 6:9
- Ephesians 5:8–9
- 2 Thessalonians 3:13

PSALM 6

HAVE COMPASSION

ON ME, LORD,

FOR I AM FAINT;

HEAL ME, LORD,

FOR MY BONES

ARE IN AGONY.

MY SOUL IS IN

DEEP ANGUISH.

HOW LONG,

O LORD,

HOW LONG?

—PSALM 6:2–3

A SONG FOR MERCY

Psalm 6 describes a person in agony. The psalmist writes: *"My soul is in deep anguish"* (v. 3). David expresses his heart-wrenching suffering and asks, *"How long, LORD?"* (v. 3). However, the end of Psalm 6 is nothing like its beginning. David feels confident that his troubles will come to an end immediately. He says, *"The LORD accepts my prayer"* (v. 9). What changed?

David's 180-degree turnabout can be explained by the first words of the psalm. Many of the psalms begin the same way: *"For the director of music."* This is generally understood to be an instruction to the conductor who would lead the music for the psalm. But the Hebrew word that begins this psalm, *"Lamenazeah,"* has another meaning as well. It means, *"For the one who has been defeated."*

Believe it or not, this term is a reference to God.

The *Talmud* teaches us that God became *"he who has been defeated"* when he "lost" the battle against Moses shortly after the people sinned by constructing a golden calf to worship. After that infamous event, God wanted to destroy the children of Israel and build a new nation from Moses. However, after much prayer and pleading, God heeded Moses' cry and relented. This is the miracle of prayer—the Almighty allows Himself to be "conquered" by mere mortals.

"Lamenazeah" is the reason that David's psalm ends on a high note. He travels from the depths of despair into the cradle of God's loving arms because he knows that his prayers have power. Psalm 6 is a gift to anyone in need. It is a ladder out of suffering, a life-saver in the midst of turbulent waters.

Today, this psalm is traditionally recited during challenging times. It's recited when someone experiences illness, or when the State of Israel is going through an unusually dangerous phase. However, this psalm can be said by anyone going through any kind of crisis.

Interestingly, we can't be sure what prompted the psalmist to write this psalm. Over the course of the psalm, he mentions several possibilities—illness, worries, and enemies. But we are left wondering which one is his focus. By leaving the exact source of his pain unclear, King David left us a useful gift: a powerful prayer to be used for all kinds of difficulties that we encounter in life.

Psalm 6 also is included in the Jewish weekday prayer service. It is at the core of a part of the service known as "supplications" or "falling on one's face." This practice, where the worshiper literally places his face down on his forearm, is based on the behavior of Moses, Aaron, and Joshua. Each one of these holy men prayed with their face on the ground when they went to beg for mercy from the Lord.

This psalm is the perfect expression of pouring out your heart to God — whatever your circumstances.

A CHRISTIAN SONG

Lord, I Can Suffer Thy Rebukes
BASED ON PSALM 6

*Lord, I can suffer
thy rebukes,*

*When thou with kindness
dost chastise;*

*But thy fierce wrath
I cannot bear:*

*O let it not
against me rise.*

—ISAAC WATTS (1674–1748)

Psalm 6

AMONG THE

DEAD NO ONE

PROCLAIMS

YOUR NAME.

WHO PRAISES

YOU FROM

THE GRAVE?

—PSALM 6:5

Only the Living

The *Talmud* teaches that when God wanted to give the *Torah* to mankind, the angels protested. They see Moses in the heavenly abode and say, "What business has a mortal among us?"

"He has come to receive the *Torah*," answers God.

"The secret treasure? You desire to give it to flesh and blood?" the angels protest.

The angels argue that human beings, with all their shortcomings, didn't deserve the gift of God's Word. They suggest that they, the perfect ones, were better suited to preserve the Word of God.

So God turns to Moses and says, "Give them an answer."

Moses responds to the angels, "What is written in the *Torah? 'I am the* LORD *your God, who brought you out of the Land of Egypt.'* Did you go down to Egypt? Were you enslaved to Pharaoh? Why then should the *Torah* be yours?

"Again, what is written in it? *'You shall have no other gods.'* Do you dwell among idol worshipers? *'Remember the Sabbath day, to keep it holy.'* Do you perform work that you need to rest? *'You shall not lie.'* Do you engage in business dealings? *'Honor your father and mother.'* Have you fathers and mothers? *'You shall not murder. You shall not commit adultery. You shall not steal.'* Is there jealousy among you? Is the Evil Tempter among you?"

Immediately the angels conceded to the Holy One, and Moses became beloved in their eyes.

This brief exchange between Moses and the angels teaches us the value of humanity. God could have made us perfect, like He created the angels.

DEVOTION

But what would be the point of life? It's no big deal to behave godly when that is your very nature. If we didn't have the temptation to do wrong, what would be meaningful about doing things right?

God doesn't want robots, God wants people. God wants us to choose goodness, to choose godliness, to choose Him. The very fact that we are prone to fall down in sin is what gives us the opportunity to ascend even higher than angels. Humankind deserves the *Torah* because only we can live its purpose.

In Psalm 6, David is saying, *I know that I am flawed. I know that I am imperfect. But Lord, that is why you sent me here to earth. If I were dead, I would be like an angel, without any free choice. How could I exalt Your name from Heaven? It is my very physicality that allows Your spirit to fill the earth. So, have mercy on me and let me live. Because only here on earth, in my imperfect human form, can I bring Your world to perfection.*

We all have faults and shortcomings. But that's nothing to be ashamed of and certainly nothing to hide from. All of the things that you have to improve upon are your spiritual curriculum for life. These are the things that you came here to perfect. They don't make you less worthy; they define your purpose in this world.

GOING DEEPER FOR CHRISTIANS

For a Christian perspective on spiritual growth, read:

- Romans 12:2

- Philippians 3:12

- James 1:3–4

PSALM 18

THEREFORE I
WILL PRAISE YOU,
LORD, AMONG THE
NATIONS; I WILL
SING THE PRAISES
OF YOUR NAME.
HE GIVES HIS KING
GREAT VICTORIES;
HE SHOWS
UNFAILING LOVE
TO HIS ANOINTED,
TO DAVID AND TO
HIS DESCENDANTS
FOREVER.

—PSALM 18:49–50

A SONG OF VICTORY

The preface to Psalm 18 attributes it to David, *"the servant of the LORD."* The Sages teach that anyone who ascribes everything to God is called a servant of the Lord. In this psalm, that is exactly what David does, and precisely who he is.

This psalm records the song that David composed *"when the LORD delivered him from the hand of all his enemies and from the hand of Saul."* Tradition teaches that David wrote this psalm at the end of his life. Most of David's years were spent fighting against Israel's worst enemies. A good part of his life was also spent trying to escape Saul, who was out to kill him. But when David writes this psalm, that's all far behind him. Here, in his old age, David reflects on the tumultuous life that he has lived, and he attributes all of his victories to the hand of the Lord.

In Psalm 18, David thanks God for *everything:* the past, the present, and the future.

Throughout the psalm, David's gratitude expands beyond his own lifetime. We are reminded of the past and catch a glimpse into the future. When the psalmist writes: *"The valleys of the*

sea were exposed and the foundations of the earth laid bare . . ." (v. 15), it is a reference to the parting of the Red Sea, an event that took place around five hundred years earlier.

David recognizes that the present is connected to the past. The exodus from Egypt was the foundation upon which his kingdom stood. Just as God used supernatural force to defeat Egypt, He interceded on David's behalf in his wars. Triumph would have been impossible without God.

At the end of the psalm, David expresses his thanks for events yet to happen. He says, *"He gives his king great victories . . . to David and to his descendants forever"* (v. 50). David understands that he is part of a chain that stretches back into the past and continues on into the future. Just as the miracles in Egypt would set the tone for his victories, his triumphs would frame Israel's ultimate victory at the End of Days. David's descendant is the Messiah, and his battles will be fought like David's—they will be supernatural, wondrous, and totally dependent upon the Almighty.

Judaism has a custom to say grace not just before meals, but also after them. The source for this is, *"When you have eaten and are satisfied, praise the LORD your God for the good land he has given you"* (Deuteronomy 8:10). The *Torah* recognizes that man has a tendency to turn toward God before his needs are met, but seems to forget about Him once he is satisfied. Saying *Grace after Meals* was instituted to avoid that pitfall. Appropriately, the last verse of Psalm 18 was chosen to be included in this grace. While some people may forget God when they are successful, King David remembers Him with eternal gratitude.

A CHRISTIAN SONG

O God, My Strength and Fortitude

BASED ON PSALM 18

My God, my Rock,
in whom I trust,

The worker of my wealth,

My Refuge, Buckler,
and my Shield,

The horn of all my health.

—THOMAS STERNHOLD
(1500–1549)

Psalm 18

THE LORD IS
MY ROCK, MY
FORTRESS AND
MY DELIVERER;
MY GOD IS MY
ROCK, IN WHOM
I TAKE REFUGE,
MY SHIELD AND
THE HORN OF MY
SALVATION, MY
STRONGHOLD.

—PSALM 18:2

The Lord Is My Rock

Just before the modern State of Israel declared her independence, there was a fierce debate. The religious Jews insisted that the name of God be included in the official Declaration of Independence document. But the secular, non-religious sector wanted religion out of it. It was Friday, May 14, and all parties wanted to be officially independent before the start of the Sabbath.

A compromise was reached. Instead of using one of the traditional names of God, He would be referred to as "the rock of Israel." This was vague enough for the non-religious, yet significant enough for the believers.

In Psalm 18, David refers to God as his rock. What does this poetic, yet ambiguous term mean? David specifies—God as his rock is his shield, horn, and stronghold.

A rock can be used as a shield. Hold a rock in front of you, and it can deflect all kinds of harmful objects. David recognizes that God is his protector when he goes out to war. In his very first fight—against the giant Goliath—King Saul tries to make David wear armor, but David refuses. Instead, he chooses to go into battle armed with the name of God.

A rock can also be a weapon. In the Scriptures, a horn is a symbol of power and might. Animals use their horns to attack. Without it, they would be powerless. David recognizes that God is his greatest weapon. In Psalm 18, David recognizes that his military victories had very little to do with him and everything to do with the Lord. Without God, he would have been crushed by King Saul long before he ever ascended the throne.

Finally, a rock, in the form of a cave, can be a stronghold. When David is hiding from King Saul, he finds a deserted cave. Saul's men are not far behind, and they find the cave, too. But they don't enter it. Why? According to Jewish tradition, God had a spider spin a web in the moments after David had entered the cave. Saul's men saw the web and assumed that no one could have possibly entered the cave recently. The physical rock may have provided the space, but God provided David's protection.

When we call God our rock, we recognize that He is our savior and protector. We recognize that without Him, we are vulnerable and exposed. How fortuitous that this became the term used in Israel's Declaration of Independence. They couldn't have picked a better name!

At the outset of the modern Israeli state, it was made clear that Israel would be independent from everyone. Everyone, that is, except God. God was, is, and always will be the rock of Israel. God is Israel's foundation, without whom, she could not stand.

Designate God as your rock. Remember that He is not far away in the distance. God is with you, protecting you and fighting your battles. Even in turbulent times, He will be your solid ground.

GOING DEEPER FOR CHRISTIANS

For a Christian perspective on God, your Rock, read:

- Matthew 16:17–19
- Luke 6:47–49
- 1 Corinthians 10:3–4

PSALM 20

MAY THE LORD

ANSWER YOU

WHEN YOU ARE

IN DISTRESS;

MAY THE NAME

OF THE GOD

OF JACOB

PROTECT YOU.

—PSALM 20:1

A SONG FOR BATTLE

Psalm 20 is a song of war. Tradition teaches that King David composed this song for his army and would recite it every time that they went out to battle. The *Talmud* teaches that because David prayed, the army was successful. Prayer was the most powerful weapon in Israel's arsenal.

Psalm 20 is made up of two parts. Verses 1–5 are requests for divine assistance. For example, we read in verse 4, *"May he give you the desire of your heart and make all your plans succeed."* Verses 6–9 are assurances that God will stand by the side of the soldiers: *"Now this I know: the LORD gives victory to his anointed"* (v. 6). David knows that God can make Israel victorious even when they are up against incredible odds. And King David should know—he was the underdog from the very first day of his career.

Remember? When David is just a boy and Saul is still king, Israel faced an enemy known as the Philistines. Goliath is their champion. No one wants to fight the 10-foot warrior, but David, a small shepherd boy, takes up the challenge. When David goes out to confront the giant, Goliath can't believe that this little kid thinks he is going to kill him with nothing more than sticks and stones.

But young David knows that he goes into battle with weaponry far superior to swords and spears. He says to Goliath, *"You are coming to fight against me with a sword, a spear and a javelin. But I'm coming against you in the name of the LORD who rules over all. He is the God of the armies of Israel. He's the one you have dared to fight against"* (1 Samuel 17:45). One slingshot later, and Goliath is dead. David sets the precedent for generations to come. Anyone who fights against Israel, fights against God.

The Sages recognize that Psalm 20 isn't only for the battlefield. Each day presents battles for every individual. David's words remind us all that we don't face our challenges alone. With God by our side, any challenge—even a giant one—is surmountable. This psalm is the very last psalm recited in the Jewish daily prayer service. Its placement is perfectly selected as we end our service and begin our day armed with prayer.

This psalm is also included when praying for the safety of the Israel Defense Forces, recognizing that prayer continues to be a vital element of Israel's success. Jewish houses of worship around the world regularly recite special prayers on behalf of the Israel Defense Forces because we know that Israel's success and survival remain dependent upon God's help. Appropriately, as 18-year-olds are inducted into the Israeli army, they are given two items—a gun and a Bible.

Both are powerful and necessary weapons upon which Israel's very existence depends.

A CHRISTIAN SONG

Now May the God of Power and Grace
BASED ON PSALM 20

*Some trust in horses
    trained for war,*

*And some of chariots
    make their boasts;*

Our surest expectations are

*From Thee, the Lord
    of heavenly hosts.*

—ISAAC WATTS (1674–1748)

Psalm 20

SOME TRUST IN

CHARIOTS AND

SOME IN HORSES,

BUT WE TRUST

IN THE NAME

OF THE LORD

OUR GOD.

—PSALM 20:7

In God We Trust

David Ben-Gurion once said, "To live in Israel, you have to believe in miracles." He was right. There is no greater military upset than Israel's victory over her enemies. The fact that Israel exists is a reminder that great miracles are still happening today.

But who is responsible for these wonders?

Israel herself is still finding out. Two of Israel's greatest battles came in quick succession of each other, but played out very differently. In 1967, Israel fought the Six-Day War. In response to a threat from the Arab world, Israel's military reacted swiftly and strongly. The whole war was won in less than a week! Jews and Israel's supporters everywhere felt both awe and pride. Perhaps a little too much pride.

Israel's slogan after the Six-Day War was "All the honor to the Israel Defense Forces." The IDF deserved credit. Indeed, Israel's army is among the best in the world. But not enough credit was given to the Lord. Scripture tells us, *"God is the one who goes with you to fight for you"* (Deuteronomy 20:4). All of Israel's battles are fought and won by the Lord.

The *Yom Kippur* War, fought in 1973, was a completely different experience for Israel. The war was unexpected; the army, unprepared. Syria attacked and outnumbered Israel. One particularly memorable battle was fought in a place now known as "The Valley of Tears," due to the loss of life during the fierce battle that took place there. The Syrians had over 1,000 tanks equipped with night-vision technology. Israel had less than 200 tanks, none of which had

DEVOTION

night-vision capability. The battle took place at night. Israel was outnumbered and ill-equipped. But guess who won? God performed great miracles, and while Israel sustained heavy casualties, she defeated her enemies.

Battles such as this one are the reason Israel's motto changed after the *Yom Kippur War*. It became "Israel trusts in God." Everyone realized that God was behind the miracle. It was no accident that the war began on *Yom Kippur*. Almost every Jew spent that day—the holiest day of the Jewish calendar—engaged in prayer and fasting. Those are the weapons that helped win the war.

In Psalm 20, the psalmist divides the world into two different types of people: those who rely on chariots, and those who rely on God. These words are not just meant for soldiers. It doesn't matter if you are up against an army, your boss, or your bank account. It all comes down to this: Do you trust in what you have—your talents, your actions, and your possessions—or do you trust in God?

More people have placed their trust in the U.S. dollar than anything else in history. But what is written on it? "In God we trust." Green paper will only go so far; God is without limits.

Place your trust in the Lord and He will fight your battles for you. You will see miracles and you will know beyond the shadow of a doubt from Whom they came.

GOING DEEPER FOR CHRISTIANS

For a Christian perspective on winning spiritual victories, read:

- John 16:33
- Romans 8:35–37
- 1 Corinthians 15:57
- 1 John 5:4–5

PSALM 23

THE LORD IS

MY SHEPHERD,

I LACK NOTHING.

HE MAKES ME LIE

DOWN IN GREEN

PASTURES, HE

LEADS ME BESIDE

QUIET WATERS,

HE REFRESHES

MY SOUL.

—PSALM 23:1–3A

A SONG OF THE SHEPHERD

Psalm 23 is arguably the most famous of all psalms. In the familiar and comforting words of the opening verses, King David compares God to a devoted shepherd who leads His sheep to lush pastures and streams of refreshing water. He makes sure that His flock is well cared for. As a sheep in God's care, David explains that he has absolutely nothing to fear. Even in the darkest and most frightening places, David will feel secure. He will take comfort in the knowledge that God is by his side.

Tradition teaches that this psalm was composed in the Forest of Hereth. David had gone there seeking asylum from King Saul, who wanted him dead. When David arrived in the forest, he discovered that it was as arid as a desert. There was no water and zero vegetation. David found himself in a brutally hot place where he would have surely perished, if not for God. The Sages tell us that God moistened the forest and provided David with ample sustenance. David responded by giving praise to God for His ability to provide for a person's needs, even in the harshest of conditions.

The Sages encourage anyone who feels anxious

about his or her current circumstances to recite, study, and ponder this psalm. The psalmist invites us to trust that the Almighty will provide us with our every need. Just as David found himself in a place of utter scarcity and there experienced extreme abundance, so can we.

The psalm comes to a close by explaining the reason for our wanting. We don't want to live so that we can eat. We want to eat so that we can live. We aren't asking for an easy life so that we can live a life of pleasure. We ask that God's *"goodness and love"* (v. 6) follow us so that we can *"dwell in the house of the Lord"* (v. 6). In other words, we ask that God provide for our needs so that we can concentrate on what we really live for: to serve God.

This is why Psalm 23 is traditionally said—or rather sung—on the Sabbath, particularly at the third meal. Out of the three meals held on the Sabbath, the third one is considered the most holy. That's because, by that time, we aren't so hungry. The first two meals we eat for ourselves. We satisfy our hunger. But the third meal is in honor of God. We demonstrate that we are deserving of God's sustenance. We desire it for the right reason—not to lead a life of luxury, but to pursue a life of spirituality.

Psalm 23 has become much more than a request for livelihood. It is a universal psalm that is recited in any time of crisis. The imagery of God as our shepherd has made this psalm the perfect companion for anyone who feels helpless and alone. Through the words of the psalm, we echo David's cry, "God, I can't do it on my own; only You can save me," and like David in the forest, we pray God will answer us with abundant blessings.

A CHRISTIAN SONG

The Lord's My Shepherd
BASED ON PSALM 23

*Yea, though I walk through
    death's dark vale,*

Yet will I fear no ill;

*For Thou art with me,
    and Thy rod*

And staff me comfort still.

—Francis Rous (1579–1659)

Psalm 23

EVEN THOUGH I
WALK THROUGH
THE DARKEST
VALLEY, I WILL
FEAR NO EVIL, FOR
YOU ARE WITH ME;
YOUR ROD AND
YOUR STAFF, THEY
COMFORT ME

—PSALM 23:4

Fear No Evil

King David speaks about "the darkest valley." There was no darker place than Poland in the middle of the 20th century. There, the brutal regime of the Nazis murdered more than 12 million innocent people, more than half of whom were Jews. While many have compared the Jews of the Holocaust to sheep going to be slaughtered—helpless and hopeless—there are many stories that prove that they were more like the sheep in David's psalm. They went as sheep in God's flock, and with the Lord as their shepherd, they had nothing to fear.

One such story took place in a forest just outside the city of Lublin. The Jews of Lublin were placed under the control of Commander Glabochnik, a notoriously sadistic murderer. He gathered all of the Jews and herded them to a field on the outskirts of the city. High barbed-wire fences surrounded it. Guards stood with machine guns and whips in hand, awaiting orders from their commander.

Glabochnik began to laugh. Then he screeched, "Sing, Jews, sing! I want you to sing a happy song!" How could the Jews sing? They defied their oppressors with silence. Then Glabochnik ordered his guards to attack. They beat and pushed the Jews into the barbed-wire fences, which tore at their flesh and blood began to flow. Again came the hideous voice: "Sing you arrogant Jews, or you will die." Suddenly, a single voice broke the silence. He began to sing a familiar Hasidic song.

"Lomir zich iberbetten, iberbetten, iberbetten,
Avinu Shebashamayim.
Lomir zich iberbetten, iberbetten, iberbetten"

DEVOTION

*"Let us reconcile, our Father
    in Heaven, let us reconcile."*

But then he changed the words.

*"Mir vellen zey iberleben,
    iberleben, iberleben,
    Avinu Shebashamayim;
    Mir vellen zey iberleben,
    iberleben, iberleben."*

"We shall outlive them, Father in Heaven, we shall outlive them."

Soon, every Jew from Lublin joined in. They were singing and then dancing. Arm in arm, heads held high, they sang in the faces of their Nazi oppressors. When Glabochnik realized that his plan had backfired—that the Jews were strengthened and not diminished by his command—he ordered them to stop. But they would not. They could not be intimidated with God by their side.

Hardly anyone survived the massacre that followed, but the Jewish people continue to live on. We are here to tell the story. In the darkest place, the Jews found light. God was with them. They had a promise that the Jewish people could never be destroyed and a promise that their souls would be bound up in everlasting life. *I will fear no evil, for you are with me.*

The Jews of Lublin left behind an eternal legacy. No matter what kind of evil you may come up against, do not fear. Sing, dance, and hold your head up high. May the Lord be with you, now and for eternity.

GOING DEEPER FOR CHRISTIANS

For a Christian perspective on God as your shepherd, read:

- Matthew 9:35–36
- John 10:1–18
- Hebrews 13:20–21
- Revelation 7:16–17

PSALM 24

WHO MAY ASCEND
THE MOUNTAIN OF
THE LORD? WHO
MAY STAND IN
HIS HOLY PLACE?
THE ONE WHO
HAS CLEAN HANDS
AND A PURE HEART,
WHO DOES NOT
TRUST IN AN IDOL
OR SWEAR BY
A FALSE GOD.

—PSALM 24:3-4

A SONG FOR GOD'S PRESENCE

Tradition teaches that King David composed Psalm 24 in honor of the occasion of bringing the Ark into the Temple. Even though the construction of the Temple would happen only after David's death during Solomon's reign, he was inspired to express his feelings about the day he knew would eventually come.

David wrote the psalm when the site of the future Temple was revealed to him. Toward the end of his reign, a great plague swept through the land. More than 70,000 people had been killed, but then the plague stopped as suddenly as it had started. The point at which the plague stopped was the place destined to be the site for the Temple.

David quickly realized the significance of the land. He purchased the

site, constructed an altar, and offered sacrifices. Then he declared that the area would be designated as the place of the Temple: *"Then David said, 'The house of the LORD is to be here'"* (1 Chronicles 22:1). It was at this point, say the Sages, that David composed this psalm. It would mark God's official entry into His earthly dwelling place.

There are three main ideas in Psalm 24. David begins by reminding us that God created the world. In the second part, David tells us that there is one place in the world that is different from any other. While all people are invited to enjoy God's world, only those who are worthy will be allowed to enter the house of the Lord. The psalm ends with a formal induction of the Ark into the Temple, and David invites the gates to open so that God, the King, can enter His palace.

Psalm 24 has earned a prominent place in Jewish liturgy. In fact, it has earned three, each connected to one of the three ideas that this psalm expresses.

In the Jewish faith, it is customary to recite one of David's psalms every day. Each day has a psalm, the *Song of the Day*, that the Sages felt was best suited for that particular day. Psalm 24 is recited every Sunday. Since Sunday was the day on which Creation began, this psalm, which recalls Creation, is a perfect fit.

Psalm 24 is also featured in the High Holy Days services. These days are designated for introspection and repentance. This psalm reminds us that it takes good character to be worthy of entrance into the house of the Lord, both on earth and in heaven. Finally, several times a week, the *Torah* is read in the synagogue. This psalm is recited as the *Torah* is returned to the Ark. While we no longer have the Temple, and therefore God's presence is no longer there, we do have His Word and we have places of worship. Just as this psalm was used to mark God's presence on earth during Temple times, we use it similarly even now. As the *Torah* is placed in the Ark, we honor God's presence and recognize His sovereignty.

A CHRISTIAN SONG

Lift Up Your Heads, Ye Mighty Gates

BASED ON PSALM 24

Lift up your heads,
　ye mighty gates,

Behold the King
　of glory waits,

The King of kings
　is drawing near,

The Saviour of
　the world is here;

Life and salvation
　doth He bring,

Wherefore rejoice,
　and gladly sing

Praise, O my God,
　to Thee!

Creator, wise
　is Thy decree!

—Catherine Winkworth
(1827–1878)

Psalm 24

LIFT UP YOUR

HEADS, YOU GATES;

BE LIFTED UP, YOU

ANCIENT DOORS,

THAT THE KING

OF GLORY MAY

COME IN.

—PSALM 24:7

This Way Up

The *Talmud* tells us that when King Solomon wanted to open the gates of the Temple, they stuck together. It was the inauguration of the Temple, and Solomon was about to place the Ark into the Holy of Holies, but he couldn't get in. So Solomon began to pray.

He prayed 24 different prayers, but the gates stubbornly refused to open. Finally, Solomon invoked the name of King David, his father, and immediately, the gates rose up. This is hinted at in Psalm 24: *"Lift up your heads, you gates; be lifted up you ancient doors."*

Why wouldn't the gates open for Solomon? And if they were stuck together, why were they raised and not separated?

The Sages teach us that Solomon's 24 prayers were offered in the merit of the people. There were 24 rotating groups of priests who would serve in the Temple. There were also 24 rotating groups of representatives who attended Temple services. The number 24 represents all types of people. Each time Solomon prayed, it was in the merit of a different type of person. But the gates wouldn't open for Solomon because no one is perfect. Nobody's merit was great enough to open the gates.

At last, Solomon prayed in the merit of his father. Why do the doors open for David? Scripture tells us of at least one sin that he committed. Surely David is not perfect!

The Sages teach that David's merit was not based on who he was; it was based on who he was becoming while on earth. King David

DEVOTION

was always becoming better. No, he was not without flaws. But he was constantly repairing them. No matter how low he had fallen, King David was constantly rising up. This is why when the gates open, they don't separate; they rise.

Rabbi Mendel of Kotzk, a 19th century Hasidic Master, once asked his students the following question: "If two people are on a ladder, and one person is on the third rung and another on the fifth, which person is higher up?" The students answered, "The person on the fifth rung." "Not necessarily," said the Rabbi. "It depends on which way they are going." Rabbi Mendel teaches that the direction in which one is moving is far more important than where that person is at the time.

King David is a master at ascending the ladder to heaven, and in the book of Psalms, he shares his tools with us. There is a psalm for every occasion, and so everything that happens to us can also elevate us. The book of Psalms doesn't make anyone perfect, but it can make everyone better.

People are called human beings, but I have found that human *becomings* would be a better term. God didn't create us so that we could remain as He made us. We were put here so that we can become better and climb higher.

What's your next step?

GOING DEEPER FOR CHRISTIANS

For a Christian perspective on becoming better, read:

- Romans 8:29

- 2 Corinthians 3:18

- Philippians 3:20–21

- 1 John 3:2

PSALM 27

I REMAIN
CONFIDENT OF
THIS: I WILL SEE
THE GOODNESS
OF THE LORD
IN THE LAND
OF THE LIVING.

—PSALM 27:13

A SONG FOR INTROSPECTION

Psalm 27 begins with a question: *"The LORD is my light and my salvation—whom shall I fear?"* (v. 1). Is there anything to be afraid of with God by my side? David answers, *"Though an army besiege me, my heart will not fear"* (v. 3). Even if he were surrounded by an army, David would feel entirely secure.

The rest of the psalm follows this theme and describes the special protection that God provides. It is a comforting psalm that seems fairly straightforward. However, a look at most Hebrew editions will reveal something mysterious in verse 13. The first word of the verse, *lule*, is written with a series of strange dots over and below it as if to call the reader's attention to that one word. Indeed, that word is the key that unlocks the full meaning of the psalm.

Verse 13 reads: *"I remain confident of this: I will see the goodness of the LORD in the land of the living."* King David is telling us he is totally confident that he will be the beneficiary of the Lord's goodness . . . but is he? The unusual dots in the beginning of this sentence have led many commentators to suggest that David is not so sure.

While David is confident that all righteous people have nothing to fear, he isn't as sure that he is counted among the righteous. David's message is this: All of the things that I have said about the Lord—that He will protect us, save us, and shower us with His goodness—are conditional! The condition, according to David, is that we are deserving of God's protection and goodness. This casts the psalm in an entirely different light: the psalm is not a promise; it's an opportunity.

In the Jewish faith, the High Holy Days are part of a time period that spans nearly two months. Jews begin preparing for *Rosh Hashanah,* the Day of Judgment, and *Yom Kippur,* the Day of Atonement, a full month before the holidays take place. This time is designated as an ideal opportunity for repentance. Every day, we blow the trumpet, or *shofar,* to wake us up from our spiritual slumber. We also read this psalm.

Out of the 150 psalms found in the book of Psalms, why was Psalm 27 chosen as the companion for the High Holy Days?

The Sages point out that *lule,* the mysterious word in our psalm, is *Elul* spelled backwards. *Elul* is the name of the month before the holidays. This psalm was destined for that time period. It is the perfect psalm for a time of introspection because it reminds us to examine our ways.

You can have it all, says the psalmist. You can have a wonderful and loving relationship with God. He can protect you and shield you from all harm. But it all depends on you. We begin each day of the holiday season with the intention of making ourselves worthy of the goodness described in this psalm.

A CHRISTIAN SONG

God is My Strong Salvation

BASED ON PSALM 27

God is my strong salvation,

What foe have I to fear?

In darkness
  and temptation,

My light, my help is near:

Though hosts
  encamp around me,

Firm to the fight I stand:

What terror
  can confound me,

With God
  at my right hand?

—JAMES MONTGOMERY
(1771–1854)

Psalm 27

ONE THING I ASK
FROM THE LORD,
THIS ONLY DO I
SEEK: THAT I MAY
DWELL IN THE
HOUSE OF THE
LORD ALL THE
DAYS OF MY LIFE,
TO GAZE ON
THE BEAUTY OF
THE LORD AND
TO SEEK HIM
IN HIS TEMPLE.

—PSALM 27:4

To Dwell in the House of the Lord

If you had one wish, what would it be? Would you ask for health? Wealth? Maybe happiness or protection? In Psalm 27, King David asks for one thing, and it's none of the things that most people would request. David's one wish is to *"dwell in the house of the LORD"* all the days of his life.

What does it mean to live in God's house?

What is a home? A home is a space that gives a context for the rest of our lives. It's where we rest and find our strength. It's where we are loved and learn to love others. A home forms us and makes us into the people that we are. Every decision that we make in our lives is deeply influenced by the place in which we reside.

When David asks to be in God's house, he isn't asking to spend his days in the Temple. Although David would have enjoyed spending all of his time in prayer and study, he was the king and he had a job to do. When David asks to be in God's house, he means that he wants God to be the context in which he lives his life. David wants God to be the source of every step that he takes and every decision that he makes. Whether he is sitting on his throne or out in the battlefield, David wants to be in the house of God.

Rabbi Mendel of Kotzk once asked his students: "Where is God?" They answered: "Everywhere!" But the Rabbi corrected them: "He is everywhere that you let Him in." Any place that we make a space for

DEVOTION

the Lord is a place in which He will reside. The whole world can be God's home if we let Him move in. God's house isn't any one place; it's a state of mind, and this is what David desires most.

As the psalmist so eloquently points out in the rest of Psalm 27, there is nothing better than to be in the house of the Lord. A life filled with godliness is a life full of goodness. That's why this is King David's most fervent request. And it is his only request because one who lives in the house of the Lord has everything.

God's home can become your home, too. It doesn't matter if you spend your days in an office or driving carpools. Any space can become a place for the Lord. If you remain honest in business, your office will be God's home. If you teach your children God's Word, your house will be God's home. Say grace before eating your meal, and then every restaurant can be a place of God.

Any space on this physical plane can be transformed into a place of spirit. If you keep an eye on God, you will see Him; God always has His eye on you, and any place that you are will be God's home, too.

GOING DEEPER FOR CHRISTIANS

For a Christian perspective on dwelling with God, read:

- John 1:14

- Ephesians 2:22

- Revelation 21:3

PSALM 29

> THE VOICE OF THE
> LORD IS POWERFUL;
> THE VOICE OF THE
> LORD IS MAJESTIC.
>
> —PSALM 29:4

A SONG OF GOD'S VOICE

Psalm 29 begins "*ascribe to the* LORD *glory and strength*." In this psalm, we recognize God's might. The psalm continues to demonstrate God's power through His mastery over nature. But there are two ways to understand this description. This psalm is either talking about the world's beginning, or it is speaking about its end. Perhaps King David is talking about both.

"*The voice of the* LORD" is a phrase repeated seven times in this psalm. This has led many commentators to believe that this psalm is a description of Creation. On each of the seven days, God created with words, "*And God said. . . .*" God's voice is mentioned seven times as a reference to the seven days of Creation. This psalm is a testimony that God created the world. The underlying message is: if God made it, He can do whatever He wants with it. This is God's strength.

But God's strength also will be demonstrated in the End Times. Another way of understanding "*the voice of the* LORD" is the many messages that He sends us through nature. Earthquakes should shake us up. Storms should rattle us. Just before the messianic era, the prophets predict that the world will experience many natural disasters. This will be God's voice urging man to repent. Nothing demonstrates God's might more than the upheaval of the natural order. Psalm 29 is a description of the upheaval that will take place before the messianic era.

This psalm was chosen as one of the seven psalms we read as we welcome the Sabbath. The Sabbath was designated as a day of rest because on the seventh day of Creation, God rested. Six days a week we create, but on the seventh day, we remember our Creator. There is only one Creator, and He is in charge of our world. Psalm 29 reminds us what the Sabbath is all about.

The Sabbath is also connected to the messianic era. Tradition teaches that, just as there are seven days in a week, there are seven millennia in our world. The seventh millennia will be "all Sabbath." It will be 1,000 years of rest and delight in the Lord. One of the psalm's last verses states, "*the LORD is enthroned as King forever*" (v. 10). After God's mastery over nature becomes obvious, He will be recognized as King.

Psalm 29 is also the sixth of the seven psalms read as the Sabbath begins. For the first five psalms, the congregation is seated, but when the sixth is read, everyone rises. Why? If we consider the Creation theme, this psalm represents the sixth day of Creation. We rise, because at the end of the sixth day, we welcome in the Sabbath, the holiest day of the week.

But if we understand this psalm as speaking about the future, then this psalm represents the sixth millennium. We rise, because at the end of the sixth millennium, we anticipate the messianic era. According to Jewish tradition, that time is now.

A CHRISTIAN SONG

Come, Thou Almighty King
BASED ON PSALM 29:2

Come, Thou
* Almighty King,*
Help us thy name to sing,
Help us to praise!
Father, all glorious,
O'er all victorious,
Come, and reign over us,
Ancient of days!

—ANONYMOUS
FROM BEFORE 1757

Psalm 29

THE LORD GIVES
STRENGTH TO
HIS PEOPLE; THE
LORD BLESSES
HIS PEOPLE
WITH PEACE.

—PSALM 29:11

The Blessing of Peace

*W*hen God wants to give Israel a gift, He gives them strength and blesses them with peace. What's the connection between strength and peace? Is the psalm telling us that the only way to achieve lasting peace is through might and strength?

Shalom is the Hebrew word for peace. Peace is such an important ideal for Jewish people that *shalom* has become the way to greet people and a way to say goodbye. It's also the last word of the priestly blessing, the *Grace after Meals*, and the *Amidah*, Judaism's central prayer. Judaism is obsessed with peace! One 18th century rabbi put it this way, "He who has peace, has everything."

Really? Is the answer to all of our problems simply the cessation of war?

While the end of all war would be nothing less than amazing, it is not peace. At least, it is not *shalom*. *Shalom* is written with the same letters as the Hebrew word *shalem*, which means whole. In Jewish thought, *shalom* means more than just the end of fighting; it means wholeness. To be at peace means to be complete.

Good fences may make good neighbors, but they do not create peace in its truest sense. Real peace is when neighbors interact with each other. It's when I can borrow a hammer from my neighbor if I can't find mine, and my neighbor knows that he can count on me to give him a ride when his car is in the shop. It's when we can sit and study the Scriptures together, and he teaches me ideas that I never would have thought of on my own. Good

DEVOTION

neighbors don't need fences. In fact, they are with each other all of the time! When one person completes the other, they are whole. They have *shalom*.

There is an interesting phenomenon when it comes to physics. Aristotle once said, "The whole is greater than the sum of its parts." This means that if one piece of wood can hold 40 pounds and another piece of wood can hold 40 pounds, then together they can hold much more than 80 pounds. Each side becomes stronger when working together. The same is true for people. When people work together, everyone becomes stronger.

God doesn't give His people strength so that they can achieve peace. It's the other way around! God gives Israel peace so that she can achieve strength. God recognizes that our greatest strength comes when we are at peace with each other.

Rabbi Shlomo Carlebach, the father of modern Jewish music, once explained that when many people talk at the same time, it's chaos. But when many people sing together, it is harmony. It's time we stop talking over each other and learn to sing together. Find your own song and add it to the symphony of life. Imagine what we could achieve if we had *shalom*.

GOING DEEPER FOR CHRISTIANS

For a Christian perspective on peace, read:

- Matthew 5:9
- Matthew 10:34
- John 14:27
- John 16:33
- Philippians 4:7
- Colossians 3:15

PSALM 30

LORD MY GOD,

I CALLED TO YOU

FOR HELP, AND YOU

HEALED ME. YOU,

LORD, BROUGHT

ME UP FROM

THE REALM OF

THE DEAD; YOU

SPARED ME FROM

GOING DOWN

TO THE PIT.

—PSALM 30:2–3

A SONG OF FORGIVENESS

In Psalm 30, King David celebrates having been rescued from dire straits. God saved him from "*the realm of the dead*" (v. 3) and turned his "*wailing into dancing*" (v. 11). What event inspired this psalm? What kind of danger was David in?

The Sages teach that David was not in any kind of physical peril. It was his soul that he worried about. There was one great stain on David's relatively pristine record—his sin with Bathsheba.

Let's review: One night, King David took a stroll on his roof. There, he saw a beautiful woman bathing on one of the rooftops below. He found out that the woman's husband was off in battle, so he summoned her to his palace. Some time after their night together, David learned that Bathsheba was pregnant. Not good.

Things went from bad to worse when David tried to cover up his adultery. He had Uriah, Bathsheba's husband, sent to the front lines, where he was sure to die. After Uriah was confirmed dead, David took Bathsheba to be his lawfully wedded wife. Everything was fine. Or so David thought.

Whom did David think he was fooling? God sent Nathan the prophet with a clear message for David: "You have sinned." David's punishment was equally clear. There would be infighting in his house and bloodshed. Also, the child born from his union with Bathsheba would die. These things were awful enough, but David worried that more divine retribution was to come. For many years after his sin, David was taunted by his enemies and by his own conscience. He was tortured by the thought that when he died, he would be judged wicked and his soul would be lost forever. David wondered if he would ever be forgiven by God.

One day, David got his answer. When Nathan told David that Solomon—his other son with Bathsheba—would be the builder of God's Temple, David knew that he had been forgiven. He was ecstatic, and he expressed his jubilation by writing Psalm 30. He wrote it for the dedication of the Temple that his son one day would build. With the inauguration of Solomon's Temple, David's enemies would be silenced and this painful chapter in David's life closed.

Today, Psalm 30 is read daily in the morning prayer service. It precedes the official start of the service. Its position is appropriate because it reminds us that the prayers we are about to offer are a substitute for the sacrifices that used to be given. It connects today's service to the service of the Temple that Solomon built. Psalm 30 also reminds us what those services are all about: To provide us a time to praise God, thank Him, and ask for what we need. But most important, they are a way for us to obtain forgiveness and bring us closer to God.

A CHRISTIAN SONG

O Lord, by Thee Delivered

BASED ON PSALM 30

O Lord, by Thee delivered,

I Thee with songs extol;

My foes Thou hast not suffered

To glory o'er my fall.

O Lord, my God, I sought Thee,

And Thou didst heal and save;

Thou, Lord, from death didst ransom,

And keep me from the grave.

—PSALTER, 1912

37

Psalm 30

YOU TURNED

MY WAILING

INTO DANCING;

YOU REMOVED

MY SACKCLOTH

AND CLOTHED

ME WITH JOY.

—PSALM 30:11

Turning Weakness into Strength

King David tells us that God turned his weeping into dancing and replaced his clothing of mourning with clothing of celebration. The Hebrew word that begins this verse is *hafachta*. *Hafachta* means much more than a change in situation; it means an absolute reversal—inside-out and upside-down. It means that the very thing that caused you sorrow has become the source of your joy.

Zadok the Kohen, a 19th century rabbi, taught that a person's greatest weakness has the potential to become his greatest strength. He said that if something brings you down, it is often that very thing that can lead you to the highest heights. The Rabbi quoted the *Talmud* which teaches that on the day that the Temple was destroyed, the Messiah was born. While this idea is not literal, it teaches us that growth is born from destruction. Our sinning is intrinsically connected to our salvation. But how?

Children often get holes in their pants, usually by their knees. These days, most people throw the pants away. But it used to be that you would put on a patch. Once the patch was sewn on, the pants were more durable than ever.

Our character is made the same way. The areas in which we are most vulnerable are the places where we can most succeed. We strengthen our weak spots and then those areas become the strongest of all.

Everyone has his or her weakness, an Achilles' heel that can bring him or her down. David was no different. The great king was humbled through his sin with Bathsheba. However, through intense introspection and prayer,

DEVOTION

he strengthened his character and patched himself up. When God forgave him for his sin, things didn't go back to the way they were. David was an entirely different person!

Through repentance, David had changed. His weak spot became his tough spot, and he was on a greater level than he had been before the sin even happened. Appropriately, while the union between David and Bathsheba had been the source of David's greatest pain, it became the source of his greatest joy. While their first son died because of David's sins, their second son lived to be the king and the builder of God's Temple. The source of David's sorrow became the reason for his joy.

The Star of David has become Judaism's most famous symbol. With one triangle pointing up and the other pointing down, the sign has many meanings. One idea is the same concept that we have been discussing. One triangle points downward. But flip that very triangle over and suddenly it points up. Bring both triangles together, and you have a star. When you take that which brings you down and flip it so that it raises you up, you shine your brightest.

As Rabbi Zadok taught, if you want to know how you can become great, look at where you are failing. What trips you up can also help you soar.

GOING DEEPER FOR CHRISTIANS

For a Christian perspective on your weaknesses, read:

- 1 Corinthians 1:27
- 2 Corinthians 11:30
- 2 Corinthians 12:9–10
- Philippians 4:12–13

PSALM 34

FEAR THE LORD,
YOU HIS HOLY
PEOPLE, FOR THOSE
WHO FEAR HIM
LACK NOTHING.
THE LIONS MAY
GROW WEAK AND
HUNGRY, BUT
THOSE WHO SEEK
THE LORD LACK NO
GOOD THING.

—PSALM 34:9–10

A SONG FOR THOSE WHO FEAR GOD

The opening verses of Psalm 34 tell us exactly when this psalm was written. In the book of 1 Samuel, we read about David's escape from King Saul. David crossed the border into Philistine territory, seeking asylum, knowing that King Saul wouldn't pursue him into enemy territory. David hoped to remain there anonymously as long as he could, but his plan fell to pieces when he was recognized immediately upon his arrival.

The Philistines realized that they had an Israeli war hero on their hands, so they brought him to their king, expecting an execution. Thinking fast, David came up with a scheme and pretended to be mentally insane. He drooled on his beard and scribbled on the walls. His plan worked; the king was sure that the madman before him could not possibly be the famed David.

David was set free and left Philistine territory unharmed. It was then that he wrote this psalm.

Most of this psalm repeats the same theme. David speaks about God's responsiveness to righteous people in their times of need: *"I sought the LORD, and he answered me; he delivered me from all my fears"* (v. 4).

Although David had devised the madman scheme on his own, he recognized that the idea itself was God's answer to his cry for help. David emphasized that anyone who embraces a life of piety will want for nothing. In David's words, fierce lions were more likely to experience hunger and food shortage than frail human beings who rely on the Lord.

While most of the psalm delivers the same message, David took a four-verse tangent. He first focused on God's care and protection of the devout, but then took a detour to teach us what it takes to become righteous and the formula, if you will, for attaining God's extra protection.

How do we become deserving of God's special attention? *"Come, my children, listen to me; I will teach you the fear of the LORD"* (v. 11). We need to become God-fearing people, and David shows us how. Fearing God requires discipline in speech, action, and thought. We need to avoid hurtful words and misconduct while pursuing good deeds and social harmony. If we do our best to take care of God's world and His children, He will most certainly take care of us.

The entire psalm can be summed up in these two verses: *"Fear the LORD, you his holy people, for those who fear him lack nothing. The lions may grow weak and hungry, but those who seek the LORD lack no good thing"* (vv. 9–10).

Fear God, and you will lack nothing. These verses were chosen to begin the very last paragraph of the *Grace after Meals*. David's message is worth remembering every time that we eat. We thank God for the food that He has provided and have faith that another meal will follow. God will take care of our physical needs as long as we take proper care of our soul.

A CHRISTIAN SONG

Through All the Changing Scenes of Life

BASED ON PSALM 34:1–9

Through all the changing scenes of life,

In trouble and in joy,

The praises of my God shall still

My heart and tongue employ.

Of his deliv'rance I will boast,

Till all that are distressed

From my example comfort take,

And charm their griefs to rest.

—TATE AND BRADY'S NEW VERSION, (1696, 1698)

Psalm 34

WHOEVER OF
YOU LOVES LIFE
AND DESIRES TO
SEE MANY GOOD
DAYS, KEEP YOUR
TONGUE FROM EVIL
AND YOUR LIPS
FROM TELLING LIES.

—PSALM 34:12–13

Who Wants Life?

*T*here is an old Jewish tale about a rabbi and a merchant who turned out to be more than an ordinary salesman. Rabbi Yannai had a study hall right near the local marketplace. One day, the story goes, a peddler was advertising a most unusual product. He claimed to have in his possession a special elixir for life.

"Who wants life?" the man called out across the marketplace. Rabbi Yannai heard the peddler and expressed interest in the product. "It's not for you," the peddler said. After several more attempts to persuade the peddler to sell him his precious product, Rabbi Yannai finally succeeded in convincing the merchant to share what he had.

When the peddler dramatically revealed to Rabbi Yannai his special elixir for life, it was none other than the Bible. He opened up to the book of Psalms and read from Psalm 34: "*Whoever of you loves life and desires to see many good days, keep your tongue from evil and your lips from speaking lies*" (vv. 12–13). Upon hearing the verses, Rabbi Yannai reacted by saying that although he had read those words hundreds of times, it was only then that he finally understood their meaning.

What? The verses seem fairly straightforward. If you want a good life, watch how you speak. What did Rabbi Yannai get that he hadn't understood before?

The peddler, who went around from town to town replaying his game, obviously knew the verses from the psalm by heart. Yet, he took out the Bible to read it out loud as if to teach Rabbi Yannai to hear the verses as

DEVOTION

if for the very first time. In this new context
Rabbi Yannai was able to appreciate the truth
and power of those words in a way that he
wasn't able to before. He knew the words, but
it wasn't until then that he fully understood
their meaning.

If we truly understood the power of our
words, we would speak in an entirely different manner than we usually
do. We would pay equally as much attention to what comes out of our
mouth as to what we put in it. If you wouldn't drink gasoline, then why
would you ever gossip? If you wouldn't eat dirt, then why would you
use vulgar language?

Just as God created the world with speech, we continue to shape our
lives with the words that we speak. If that's true, how could we ever dare
to breathe a word of evil, negativity, or lies? The secret to a good life is to
speak only good words!

Simple? Yes. Easy? No. Worth it? Definitely.

Try this: Commit yourself to one or several specific hours each day in
which you are completely mindful of every word that you say. Only speak
words of truth and goodness. No gossip, no negativity, and no lies (not even
white ones). Slowly increase the hours per day that you do this, and marvel
at how your life improves!

GOING DEEPER FOR CHRISTIANS

For a Christian perspective
on the power of your
words, read:

- Matthew 12:36–37
- Matthew 15:18–20
- Ephesians 4:25
- Colossians 3:8–9
- James 3:7–12

PSALM 48

AS WE HAVE
HEARD, SO WE
HAVE SEEN
IN THE CITY
OF THE LORD
ALMIGHTY,
IN THE CITY
OF OUR GOD:
GOD MAKES HER
SECURE FOREVER.

—PSALM 48:8

A SONG ABOUT GOD'S CITY

Psalm 48 is a glorious song about Jerusalem. It is part of a group of 12 that were composed by three men known as the Sons of Korah. Who were these men?

Korah is familiar to us from Numbers, Chapter 16. It is a sad episode in the Bible, one in which many people lost their lives. Here is what happened: Korah was unhappy with how things were structured in the nation of Israel. He felt that Moses and Aaron were way out of line in keeping all the powers of leadership to themselves.

So Korah enlisted the support of 250 men, and together they began a rebellion against Moses. Their goal was to strip Moses and Aaron of their leadership and distribute it among themselves. When confronted by Korah's men, Moses told them, "This wasn't my idea, it was the Lord's." Moses, whom the

Bible calls the most humble of men, had no desire for power or honor. He reminded Korah that he himself was from the prestigious tribe of Levi—the tribe of priests. Korah already filled a privileged role! But that wasn't enough for Korah and his followers. They agreed to meet Moses and Aaron for a showdown to determine God's chosen.

The next day, Korah and his followers prepared to bring offerings to God. So did Aaron. Everyone agreed that the offerings that were accepted would determine who God preferred to lead His people. Just as the contest was about to begin, God opened up the ground and it swallowed Korah, his family, and all of his possessions. While everyone was still catching their breath, a fire came down from heaven and consumed all of Korah's followers.

God left no doubt about whom He had chosen and whom He had not.

The Sages teach that the Sons of Korah in the book of Psalms are the sons of Korah from Numbers. They were originally part of Korah's rebellion, but repented. When the earth opened to swallow them, they miraculously survived, as it says, "*The line of Korah, however, did not die out*" (Numbers 26:11). They authored powerful psalms that were passed down all the way to David.

Today, Psalm 48 is the *Song of the Day* for Monday, the second day of Creation. It is recited just after the official conclusion of the Jewish morning prayer service every Monday of every week. On the second day of Creation, God separated the waters and formed heaven and earth. Heaven is where God would reside, and His creations would live on earth. Psalm 48 teaches about a similar separation. God distinguished between the city of Jerusalem and everywhere else. Jerusalem will become God's dwelling place, from where He will rule over every continent. Just as heaven is on a higher plane than earth, Jerusalem is elevated over every other city in the world.

In this psalm, the Sons of Korah fixed their father's mistake. While Korah fought against God's order, his children sing a joyous song about it.

A CHRISTIAN SONG

How Great Thou Art
BASED ON PSALM 48:1

O Lord my God, When I in awesome wonder,

Consider all the worlds Thy Hands have made;

I see the stars, I hear the rolling thunder,

Thy power throughout the universe displayed.

Then sings my soul, My Saviour God, to Thee,

How great Thou art, How great Thou art.

Then sings my soul, My Saviour God, to Thee,

How great Thou art, How great Thou art!

—CARL GUSTAV BOBERG
(1859–1940)

Psalm 48

GREAT IS THE
LORD, AND MOST
WORTHY OF PRAISE,
IN THE CITY OF
OUR GOD, HIS
HOLY MOUNTAIN.
BEAUTIFUL IN
ITS LOFTINESS,
THE JOY OF THE
WHOLE EARTH, LIKE
THE HEIGHTS OF
ZAPHON IS MOUNT
ZION, THE CITY OF
THE GREAT KING.

—PSALM 48:1–2

Joy of the Whole Earth

Psalm 48 begins with a description of the *"city of our God."* God's city, of course, is the city of Jerusalem. There is something special about Jerusalem. The psalmist calls it *"the joy of the whole earth."* What is the source of Jerusalem's joy?

Jacob got it right when he first encountered Jerusalem. At that time Jacob was on the run, escaping his brother Esau and looking for a place to spend the night. He found a good spot, gathered a bunch of rocks together to make a pillow for his head, and went to sleep. That night, he had his famous dream of a ladder, stretching all the way from earth to the heavens. On it, he saw angels going up and down, entering and leaving the earthly realm. When Jacob woke up he said, "Oh no! This place is the entrance to God's house!"

Jerusalem is the city designated for God's Temple, His earthly home. When the Temple stood, anyone who came there would have a profound experience with the Creator. God's presence was manifest there like no other place and time on earth. The Temple reached beyond this world. It was a ladder up to heaven, and Jerusalem was the earth it rested on.

Although the Temple no longer stands, Jerusalem remains a portal between heaven and earth. The Sages teach that all prayers ascend to heaven through Jerusalem and that all blessings come down through her. Jerusalem is where all Creation began and where history will come to a close. A visit to Jerusalem is still a life-changing encounter with the Divine. Eli Weisel, the famous Holocaust survivor and Nobel laureate, put it this way: "Jerusalem:

DEVOTION

the city which miraculously transforms man into pilgrim; no one can enter it and go away unchanged."

Jerusalem is the meeting place between God and humans, and that is the source of her joy. The name Jerusalem is made up of two words—*Yeru*, "he will see," and *shalem*, "wholeness." Together they form *Yerushalyim*, the Hebrew word for Jerusalem. In Jerusalem, we encounter God, and that experience leaves us feeling complete.

Real joy is not the experience of having fun. It's the feeling of contentment that comes with wholeness. In Jerusalem, we can put back together the parts of us that have been shattered and broken. We can become complete again. When Jacob spent the night in Jerusalem on a pillow of stones, he woke up in the morning to find that all of the rocks had miraculously become one. Jerusalem makes everything whole.

Some people seek out joy by filling their lives with things. But others find happiness by filling their lives with God. True joy comes when God completes us. But you don't need an airplane to visit Jerusalem. When you fill your life with God and let Him heal your soul, you will have already been there.

GOING DEEPER FOR CHRISTIANS

For a Christian perspective on Jerusalem, God's city, read:

- Matthew 23:37
- John 4:21–23
- Galatians 4:25–26
- Hebrews 12:22
- Revelation 3:12
- Revelation 21:2

PSALM 49

PEOPLE, DESPITE
THEIR WEALTH,
DO NOT ENDURE;
THEY ARE LIKE
THE BEASTS
THAT PERISH.

—PSALM 49:12

A SONG ABOUT TRUE WEALTH

As upbeat and joyful as Psalm 48 is, Psalm 49 is somber and solemn. It is a reflection upon wealth and its ultimate futility: "*People, despite their wealth, do not endure; they are like the beasts that perish*" (v. 12). Every life comes to an end, and at that time, all of the money in the world isn't worth anything.

Psalm 49 is one of the 12 psalms written by Korah's sons. According to Jewish tradition, they were composed between the time when Korah's sons were swallowed by the earth and when they climbed out. The men were miraculously sheltered underground while everyone else around them perished. As they sat between worlds, they absorbed everything that had happened. In those powerful moments of clarity, they wrote these psalms. When we read the psalms of Korah's sons and remember the conditions under which they were written, these psalms take on a whole new depth of meaning.

Korah was an extremely wealthy man. Even today, there is an expression in Hebrew used to describe an affluent person: "as rich as Korah." The *Talmud* says that hundreds of mules were needed just to carry the keys to Korah's treasure houses! Legend has it that Korah was one of the wealthiest people to ever live.

In the book of Ecclesiastes, King Solomon wrote, "*I have seen a grievous evil under the sun: wealth hoarded to the harm of its owners*" (Ecclesiastes 5:13). The Sages explain that the wealth in this verse—the kind that hurts its owners—is a reference to the wealth of Korah. Korah's wealth gave him a false sense of security and caused him to think that he was greater than he really was. But Korah's wealth ended up his greatest enemy. It led to his rebellion, and ultimately, his downfall. He was left not only penniless, but also without any merit.

Korah's sons witnessed their powerful father reduced to nothingness. Their thoughts became the words of this psalm: "*This is the fate of those who trust in themselves, and of their followers . . . Their forms will decay in the grave, far from their princely mansions*" (vv. 13–14). Korah's sons had seen what happens to those who are haughty because of their wealth: they rot in their grave and their possessions can't help them. "*The ransom for a life is costly, no payment is ever enough*" (v. 8). No amount of money can buy back a life.

Psalm 49 puts money in its place and gives us all perspective. This psalm is traditionally recited in the house of mourners. In Jewish tradition, mourners observe *shiva*, the practice of mourning the loss of a close relative for seven days. During that time period, friends and family come to visit. They remember the deceased and give comfort to the bereaved. *Shiva* is also meant to have an impact upon the visitors. We read this psalm in hopes that the death of one person can inspire others to live more powerfully and with better clarity.

A CHRISTIAN SONG

In Vain the Wealthy Mortals Toil
BASED ON PSALM 49:9

*In vain the wealthy
  mortals toil,*

*And heap their shining
  dust in vain,*

*Look down and scorn
  the humble poor,*

*And boast their lofty hills
  of gain.*

—Isaac Watts (1674–1748)

Psalm 49

DO NOT BE
OVERAWED WHEN
OTHERS GROW
RICH, WHEN THE
SPLENDOR OF
THEIR HOUSES
INCREASES; FOR
THEY WILL TAKE
NOTHING WITH
THEM WHEN
THEY DIE, THEIR
SPLENDOR WILL
NOT DESCEND
WITH THEM.

—PSALM 49:16–17

The Value of Money

The Rothschild family is one of the most famous banking families in the world. They also happen to be Jewish. Over the generations, many stories have been passed down about this prominent family. No one knows for sure which are true, but that doesn't take away from their message and meaning.

One well-known story is about how the Rothschilds became wealthy. In the mid-18th century, Mayer Amschel Rothschild was an attendant for Rabbi Hirsch, the local clergyman. Once he got married, Mayer Amschel left his position with the Rabbi and opened his first store. It became an instant success.

Soon after, the Rabbi's daughter became engaged. When the Rabbi went to take the money that he had saved as her dowry, it was missing! The entire family was sure that Mayer Amschel had taken the 500 ducats to start his store. The Rabbi reluctantly approached Mayer Amschel with the accusation. Mayer Amschel looked at the Rabbi and said, "They are right. I took the money. I only have 200 ducats now, but I will return the rest as soon as possible." The Rabbi was disappointed in his former attendant, but soon all of the money was returned.

A few months later, Rabbi Hirsch got a surprise. The governor needed to see him immediately. When he arrived, the governor told him that the local officials had recovered 500 ducats from a thief and had traced the origins of the money to the Rabbi's house. The governor handed the Rabbi a sack. In it was the money that he had discovered missing months ago.

The Rabbi realized immediately that Mayer Amschel had never stolen the money and that he had lied when he said that he did. He rushed over

DEVOTION

to Mayer Amschel and showered him with apologies. But the Rabbi had a question, too.

"Why did you do it? Why didn't you defend your innocence?" he asked. Mayer Amschel answered, "I saw how much you needed the money. At that moment, helping you out mattered more than my money or my reputation." The Rabbi gave Mayer Amschel a blessing that he would become wealthy, because clearly, he understood the value of money. Evidently, the blessing was fulfilled.

More recently, someone asked one of the Rothschilds, "Exactly how much wealth do you have?" In response, Lord Rothschild answered, "Let me show you." He led the man to a room and showed him many documents — all receipts from charitable donations he had made. "These," said Lord Rothschild, "are my only true possessions. Only the money that I have given away will accompany me to the grave."

The psalmist warns us not to get blinded by wealth. Don't be awed when someone else becomes extremely wealthy, the psalm says, "*For they will take nothing with them when they die.*" All possessions are meaningless in the end; only our good deeds will be with us forever. These are words to live by—and also by which to die.

GOING DEEPER FOR CHRISTIANS

For a Christian perspective on true treasure and money, read:

- Matthew 6:19–20
- Matthew 19:21–23
- 1 Timothy 6:9–10
- James 5:1–6

PSALM 51

RESTORE TO ME

THE JOY OF YOUR

SALVATION AND

GRANT ME A

WILLING SPIRIT TO

SUSTAIN ME. THEN

I WILL TEACH

TRANSGRESSORS

YOUR WAYS, SO

THAT SINNERS

WILL TURN

BACK TO YOU.

—PSALM 51:12–13

A SONG OF REPENTANCE

There are only a few psalms that tell us when they were composed. Psalm 51 is one of them. Yet, from all of the psalms that David penned, this would be the one to keep discreet. The introductory verse tells us that this psalm was composed just after David had sinned with Bathsheba. Why does David air his dirty laundry? Why does he share his failure with the world?

King David understood very well who he was and what role he would play in the future of humanity. By opening up this painful chapter for everyone to read, David invites us to learn from his mistakes. Toward the end of the psalm, David wrote: "*Then I will teach transgressors your ways, so that sinners will turn back to you*" (v. 13). Ever the leader, David used his transgression as a lesson for us all.

The first part of the psalm teaches us about repentance. The second part teaches about prayer. Both are critical components when returning to God. Through them, one can be cleansed of sin. As the psalmist wrote, "*I will be whiter than snow*" (v. 7).

In Psalm 51, David did three things as part of his

repentance: he confessed his sin, expressed regret, and resolved to avoid the sin in the future. This three-step approach has remained the system of repentance through today, and this psalm has become a companion for every repentant person.

In verse 11, David begged God for a second chance: "*Do not cast me from your presence . . .*" This verse has become prominent in the High Holy Days experience. Special prayers of confession are recited every morning the week before *Rosh Hashanah*, and they are also recited on the High Holy Days themselves (the ten days between the start of *Rosh Hashanah* and *Yom Kippur*). At that time, verse 11 takes center stage. It captures our feelings as we stand in judgment before God. We pray that our sins be forgiven and our judgment favorable.

The second part of Psalm 51 is a lesson in prayer. The psalmist wrote: "*My sacrifice. . . is a broken spirit; a broken and contrite heart you, God, will not despise*" (v. 17). In place of bringing sacrifices, David offered his heart. This broken spirit and absolute surrender to God is the key to prayer. Such a heart *"God will not despise"* (v. 17). Only a person who is broken before God can make him or herself whole again.

Every Jewish prayer service centers around one central prayer known as the *Amidah*. It begins with this verse: "*Open my lips, Lord, and my mouth will declare your praise*" (v. 15). When we understand the psalm from which the verse was taken, we can understand the meaning of the words. David spoke these words just after he recognized the enormity of his sin. He was too broken to speak and so he asked that God would help open his lips. It is this spirit of brokenness that we try to recapture every single time that we pray. With David's broken spirit, we hope to reclaim our own.

A CHRISTIAN SONG

Create in Me A Clean Heart

BASED ON PSALM 51:10–12

Create in me a clean heart,
    O God,

and renew a right spirit
    within me.

Create in me a clean heart,
    O God,

and renew a right spirit
    within me.

Cast me not away from
    your presence, O Lord,

and take not your Holy
    Spirit from me.

Restore unto me the joy
    of your salvation,

and renew a right spirit
    within me.

—ANONYMOUS

Psalm 51

CREATE IN ME

A PURE HEART,

O GOD,

AND RENEW A

STEADFAST SPIRIT

WITHIN ME.

—PSALM 51:10

A New Spirit

Renewal is a theme that runs throughout Jewish tradition. Every year is celebrated with recommitment and re-evaluation on *Rosh Hashanah*. Every new moon is observed with a festive day on the first of every month. Even the end of every week is seen as a chance to rejuvenate with the observance of the Sabbath. We are constantly sweeping out the old and stale in order to make room for the fresh and new.

A story told about the Rabbi of Salant shows us just how seriously we need to take the value of newness. The Rabbi was at a wedding where the hosts had hired an entertainer. His job was to put on an act that would get everyone laughing. The entertainer timidly approached the Rabbi and asked if it would be all right if he imitated the great Rabbi during the sketch. The Rabbi was known for his unusually high and squeaky voice. The Rabbi said, "Sure! Anything for the bride and groom!"

But when the entertainer put on the skit, the Rabbi suddenly started to cry! The entertainer felt horrible and rushed over to the Rabbi as soon as he was done. "Rabbi, I'm so sorry that I offended you! But I did ask your permission!" said the man. "I'm not crying because you offended me," replied the Rabbi. "I'm crying because you did such a good job impersonating me. And I thought—if you can imitate me so well, how much more so I can imitate myself! That's why I'm crying!"

The holy Rabbi realized just how easy it is to slip into a routine devoid of meaning. People are creatures of habit. But even a life of good habits

DEVOTION

becomes stale if those habits are done by rote. We need to renew our spirit every single day.

Abraham, the spiritual seeker who encountered the living God, described himself this way: "*I am nothing but dust and ashes*" (Genesis 18:27). This was more than a display of humility. Abraham was saying that he is constantly destroying who he is in order to become someone new. The Abraham of yesterday didn't make it to see the next sunrise. With every dawn an entirely new creation, a new man, was born.

In Psalm 51, we see David praying for renewal. He asked for a new heart and a new spirit. After his sin with Bathsheba, David needed renewal more than ever. His fervent request was for help in destroying who he was and becoming someone different. David teaches us the power of renewal. We don't need to be stuck in the past. Every moment is a chance to be someone new.

Why not begin each day by checking in with our spiritual selves? Are we choosing who we are today, or are we just imitating who we were yesterday? A life filled with genuine spirituality is never the same as the day before. We are constantly growing and changing, ever fresh and new.

GOING DEEPER FOR CHRISTIANS

For a Christian perspective on spiritual renewal, read:

- Romans 12:2
- 2 Corinthians 5:17
- Ephesians 4:23–24
- Colossians 3:10

PSALM 81

SING FOR JOY

TO GOD OUR

STRENGTH;

SHOUT ALOUD

TO THE GOD

OF JACOB!

BEGIN THE

MUSIC, STRIKE

THE TIMBREL, PLAY

THE MELODIOUS

HARP AND LYRE.

—PSALM 81:1–2

A SONG OF SONGS

For over two millennia, Psalm 81 has been recited by Jews around the world every Thursday. It is attributed to a man named Asaph, *"For the director of music . . . Of Asaph."* Who was Asaph and what is his song doing in King David's book? And why was his psalm chosen from all of the others to be one of the seven recited every week?

While we typically attribute the book of Psalms to King David, he didn't compose all 150. Tradition teaches us that among the writers included in Psalms are Adam, Abraham, and Moses. However, it was King David who brought the psalms to life. It was David who used them fervently as a way of connecting to the Lord. It was he who put them to music and gave them their soul. David may not have written all of the psalms, but he was the one who gave them a voice.

When David was compiling the book of Psalms, he had a group of poets and singers who participated, the most prominent of which was Asaph. A member of the Levite tribe, Asaph personally authored 12 psalms. In the book of Ezra, we find that the children of Asaph were among those who returned to Israel 70 years after the destruction of the First Temple, when the exiles were finally allowed to come home. There, Asaph's family is referred to as the "singers," continuing their ancestor's legacy.

Today, every Jewish morning prayer service ends with a particular psalm known as the *Song of the Day*. The psalm for each day has a deep connection to the day on which it is recited. Asaph's Psalm 81 was chosen as a fitting tribute to Thursday, the fifth day of Creation.

On the first Thursday of the world, God created the birds and the fish. The Sages explain that birds and fish lead us to praise God. The sight of so many different species covering the entire expanse of the earth, from the highest levels of the atmosphere to the deepest recesses of the sea, causes a person to appreciate the greatness of our Creator. So, each Thursday, we recognize our bountiful blessings.

Psalm 81 is the perfect choice. The psalm begins, "*Sing for joy to God our strength . . . play the melodious harp and lyre*" (vv. 1–2). It is all about recognizing God as the source of all blessings and knowing that He is capable of blessing us beyond our wildest imaginations. Asaph reminds us that when we acknowledge the One who gives, we become those who receive— immeasurably.

A CHRISTIAN SONG

Honey in the Rock

BASED ON PSALM 81:16

Oh, there's honey in the Rock, my brother;

There's honey in the Rock for you.

Leave your sins for the Blood to cover;

There's honey in the Rock for you.

—FREDERICK GRAVES
(1856–1927)

Psalm 81

YOU SHALL HAVE

NO FOREIGN GOD

AMONG YOU;

YOU SHALL NOT

WORSHIP ANY GOD

OTHER THAN ME.

I AM THE LORD

YOUR GOD, WHO

BROUGHT YOU

UP OUT OF EGYPT.

OPEN WIDE YOUR

MOUTH AND

I WILL FILL IT.

—PSALM 81:8–9

Ask and You Shall Receive

True Story. A friend of mine was feeling pretty down one day when she had one of those encounters with a human being that leaves you feeling like you've really had an exchange with a messenger from God. She was filling up her car at a gas station when a homeless man named Daniel approached her. Daniel handed her a rose that he had made from palm fronds and said, "If you have a dollar I'd appreciate it. If you don't because you only have a credit card, it's OK; it's yours."

My friend didn't have a dollar so she took out a twenty and folded it up so he wouldn't see what it was. But somehow, even folded, Daniel knew that it was more than a dollar. He said, "You know, the Almighty takes care of my needs. I never have to ask for my needs, but if I want something I have to ask. Today I asked for a bath and a place to sleep, because I didn't have either last night. And then He sent me you."

In Psalm 81:8–9, the psalmist shares with us the secret to getting what we want. These verses can be broken down into three main ideas. First, "*You shall have no foreign god . . .*" Don't think that anything or anybody in the world can help you like God can. Don't worship money or human beings because it seems that they run the show. There is nothing and no one more powerful than God. Period.

Second, "*I am the LORD . . . who brought you out of Egypt.*" Not only is the Lord the most powerful source in the universe, He is willing and able to wield His power on your behalf. Just as He rescued the children of Israel from Egypt, He can and will help you, too.

And finally, "*Open your mouth wide and I will fill it.*" Once you acknowledge that God is the source of all blessings in your life, all you have to do is open your mouth in prayer and ask Him for what you want. If what you ask for is in your best interest, God will fill your request with joy and love in exactly the right time—just as He did for Daniel.

GOING DEEPER FOR CHRISTIANS

For a Christian perspective on coming boldly to God with your requests and needs, read:

- Mark 11:24
- Luke 11:9–10
- John 14:13–14
- 1 John 3:21–22

PSALM 82

THE 'GODS'
KNOW NOTHING,
THEY UNDERSTAND
NOTHING. THEY
WALK ABOUT IN
DARKNESS; ALL
THE FOUNDATIONS
OF THE EARTH
ARE SHAKEN.

—PSALM 82:5

A SONG ABOUT JUSTICE

Asaph is the composer of Psalm 82, a song about justice. In this psalm, Asaph bemoaned corrupt judges and stressed the importance of a strong justice system in order to maintain a healthy world. He wrote, "*The 'gods' know nothing, they understand nothing. They walk about in darkness; all the foundations of the earth are shaken*" (v. 5). The judges, who thought they were like gods, were completely blind to the truth. The lack of justice threatened the very foundations of the earth.

The Sages have suggested that this psalm refers to a specific time period many years after Asaph lived. They point to the period of reign by the fourth king of Judah, Jehoshaphat. Jehoshaphat was celebrated as a good king who enacted a lot of reform in his kingdom. As part of this reform, Jehoshaphat got rid of corrupt judges and replaced them with new ones. To these men he instructed: "*Consider carefully what you do, because you are not judging for mere mortals but for the LORD . . . with the LORD our God there is*

no injustice or partiality or bribery" (2 Chronicles 19:6–7). Jehoshaphat, whose name means "God is Judge," put Asaph's words into action. He uprooted corruption and replaced it with justice.

Whether or not this psalm refers to a specific time period doesn't take away from its general message: The world cannot endure without a foundation of truth and justice. A society based on lies cannot stand.

The generation of Noah is a case in point. We read in Genesis 6, "*God saw how corrupt the earth had become, for all the people on earth had corrupted their ways. So God said to Noah, 'I am going to put an end to all people. . . . I am surely going to destroy both them and the earth'*" (vv.12–13). A world of anarchy and corruption surely is headed for destruction.

Psalm 82 is included in the group of psalms designated as the *Song of the Day*. This psalm is read at the conclusion of Tuesday morning's prayer service. On Tuesday, the third day of Creation, God created land and sea. He did this by creating boundaries for the water which, at first, covered everything. Until that moment, all earth was submerged under water and completely uninhabitable. When God cleared the water away, human beings would be able to live on land.

The connection between Psalm 82 and our prayer service on Tuesday gives us an important message—one worth remembering once a week. A world filled with corruption is just as damaging as a world flooded with water. It's not fit for human life. Appropriately, when God wanted to destroy the generation that was filled with injustice—Noah's generation—He brought about their end with a flood. Justice is as essential to our existence as dry land. Our duty is to protect the innocent from the wicked, just as God protects the land from the raging waters of the sea.

A CHRISTIAN SONG

We Give Thee But Thine Own

BASED ON PSALM 82:3

*We give Thee but
  Thine own,*

Whate'er the gift may be:

*All that we have is
  Thine alone,*

A trust, O Lord, from Thee.

May we Thy bounties thus

As stewards true receive,

*And gladly, as Thou
  blessest us,*

To Thee our first-fruits give.

—WILLIAM WALSHAM HOW
(1823–1897)

Psalm 82

DEFEND THE

WEAK AND THE

FATHERLESS;

UPHOLD THE CAUSE

OF THE POOR AND

THE OPPRESSED.

RESCUE THE WEAK

AND THE NEEDY;

DELIVER THEM

FROM THE HAND

OF THE WICKED.

—PSALM 82:3–4

Beyond the Law

When O.J. Simpson was brought to trial on charges of murder, it was called the trial of the century. The high-profile athlete was accused of slaying his former wife, Nicole Brown, and her friend, Ron Goldman. The evidence appeared overwhelming, and most of America was sure that he had committed the crime. But the trial resulted in O.J.'s acquittal, leaving many people to question our system of law.

Justice is a fundamental value in the Bible. It is mentioned many times, but there is one place that it is mentioned twice in a row: "*Follow justice and justice alone, so that you may live and possess the land the* LORD *your God is giving you*" (Deuteronomy 16:20). What is the meaning of "*justice and justice*"? Wouldn't it have been enough to write the word once?

The Sages explain that there are two types of justice. This verse commands us to uphold both. The first type of justice is the enforcement of law. We are to set up courts and conduct fair trials. We are to punish the bad guys and protect the good people. This is the basic foundation of every society.

But there is another type of justice—one that goes beyond the law. Psalm 82 reminds us that the goal of justice is not adherence to the law; it's the adherence to the values that the law aims to protect. Defend the weak, the orphans, the poor, and oppressed, says the psalmist. Keep the

wicked off the streets. The second kind of justice is the enforcement of what is right, even if it isn't strictly the law.

Where does that lead us as individuals if we do not work in the legal system? The answer is that we can practice the two types of justice in our own private lives.

The first kind of justice goes without saying. We must be fair and just in all our dealings. But we can uphold the second kind of justice, too. When we judge the people in our lives, we need to see beyond what is strictly wrong and right. We need to see people in the context of everything else. Yes, technically speaking, we may be correct. But is my friend going through a hard time right now? Can I judge her with mercy? Or when an elderly parent says something wrong and hurtful, can I excuse it because he is weak?

God wants us to exercise justice in all parts of His world. That way, we can strengthen the foundation which supports all humanity.

GOING DEEPER FOR CHRISTIANS

For a Christian perspective on justice, read:

- Matthew 23:23

- 2 Corinthians 7:10–11

- Revelation 19:11

PSALM 92

FOR YOU MAKE
ME GLAD BY
YOUR DEEDS, LORD;
I SING FOR JOY AT
WHAT YOUR HANDS
HAVE DONE. HOW
GREAT ARE YOUR
WORKS, LORD,
HOW PROFOUND
YOUR THOUGHTS!

—PSALM 92:4–5

A SONG FOR THE SABBATH

Like many other psalms, Psalm 92 was not written by King David. According to Jewish tradition, it was written by none other than the first man who ever lived—Adam.

Adam was very busy on the day that he was created. He was born, met his spouse, got his very first commandment, broke his only commandment, and was reproached by God. Tradition teaches that Adam thought that he had permanently destroyed the world with his sin. When the sun went down that night, Adam had never seen a sunset before. He was sure that the world was coming to an end. He and Eve spent the whole night crying tears of remorse. When the sun came up in the morning, they were overjoyed. They correctly assumed that sunrises and sunsets were part of life.

If Adam thought that sunset meant the world's destruction because of his sin, then why didn't he think that sunrise meant a renewal of creation because of his repentance? The answer is that Adam didn't yet know what repentance was or that it even existed. His son Cain would be the one to teach him.

Fast forward. Cain had just murdered his brother Abel. He appeared before the heavenly tribunal for judgment and left elated. The Sages record the conversation with his father that followed: "What happened in there?" asked Adam. "Why are you so happy? Don't you know that you deserve to die?"

Cain replied, "I repented and was spared from death." At that point, Adam started banging himself on the head and said, "Repentance is so powerful, and I never knew it!" It was at that moment the gift of repentance was revealed to humanity. It is also then that Adam composed our psalm.

The introductory words to Psalm 92 read: "*A psalm. A song. For the Sabbath day.*" But what does the Sabbath have to do with this newly discovered repentance? And if the psalm is about the Sabbath, then why isn't the Sabbath mentioned in any part of the psalm?

The answer is that Adam wasn't referring to the Sabbath that's celebrated every week; he was referring to the Sabbath at the end of time. In the Jewish tradition, the messianic era is considered one long Sabbath. It will be a time of peace, harmony, and perfection. When Adam discovered repentance, he realized that it was possible to fix the world and return it to the way it was before he sinned. He was ecstatic and composed this psalm — about a time in the future that will be just like the world was when it was first created.

Today, Psalm 92 is read every week on the Sabbath because every "small" Sabbath is a taste of the Great Sabbath to come. Every week, we make one day like the Garden of Eden. We focus on God, family, and everything good in the world. We remember what life was like in the beginning of time and what it can be like once again.

It Is a Good Thing to Give Thanks Unto the Lord

BASED ON PSALM 92

It is a good thing to give thanks unto the Lord

and to sing praises unto thy Name, O Most Highest;

To tell of thy loving-kindness early in the morning

and of thy truth in the night season;

Upon an instrument of ten strings and upon the lute,

upon a loud instrument and upon the harp.

For thou, Lord, hast made me glad through thy works

and I will rejoice in giving praise for the operations of thy hands.

Glory be to the Father and to the Son and to the Holy Ghost;

As it was in the beginning is now, and ever shall be, world without end.

Amen.

—THE HYMNAL
(REVISED 1892)

Psalm 92

IT IS GOOD TO

PRAISE THE LORD

AND MAKE MUSIC

TO YOUR NAME,

O MOST HIGH,

PROCLAIMING

YOUR LOVE IN

THE MORNING

AND YOUR

FAITHFULNESS

AT NIGHT.

—PSALM 92:1–2

God's Faith

*I*n Psalm 92, we are encouraged to praise the Lord, *"proclaiming your love in the morning and your faithfulness at night."* Why should we praise God differently in the morning than in the night?

The usual understanding of this verse is that the morning represents the good times in our lives when everything is bright and sunny, fresh and new. In those wonderful times, it is important to give thanks and recognize God's abundant and apparent love for us. The night, on the other hand, represents the dark times in our lives, when everything looks bleak and uncertain. In those trying moments, we express our faith in God that He will carry us through until tomorrow's sunrise.

In the midst of the Holocaust, a saintly rabbi explained the verse differently. In one of the darkest nights that the world has ever experienced, the rabbi gave a message of hope. He said, "The verse says '*Your faithfulness,*' meaning God's faith, not our faith. It's not our faith in God that gets us through the night; it's His faith in us." When the night is so dark and endless, what keeps us going is remembering how much God believes in us.

Sometimes we feel like giving up. Life is tough, and we feel defeated. But the rabbi's message tells us that if we are still here, it's because God believes in us. We have a mission and we are up to the task. If not, we would not be here.

Rabbi Shlomo Carlebach, a *Torah* scholar and song composer of the 20th century, would often perform in prison. He would greet all of

DEVOTION

the prisoners with a warm hug and invite them to join the concert. One time, after the concert had finished, one of the toughest-looking prisoners called after him, "Rabbi Carlebach, Rabbi Carlebach, could I get another hug?" Rabbi Carlebach smiled kindly and gave him a big hug. The harsh features of the prisoner softened and he said, "You know, Rabbi, if someone would have given me a hug like this 25 years ago, I wouldn't have ended up in a place like this."

It is so critical to feel that someone loves us and believes in us. It gives us the encouragement to keep going in the right direction. God is loving us and hugging us all the time. Rabbi Carlebach later said, "Everybody believes in God, hopefully. But do you know how much God believes in us? The world still exists. That means God believes in us; believes we can fix everything."

If you ever doubt your self-worth, remember that God thinks that you are invaluable. Of all the souls that He could have sent down to earth at exactly this time, He chose you. Even though the night is long and dark, God believes that together, we can bring the morning.

If God believes in us, shouldn't we, too?

GOING DEEPER FOR CHRISTIANS

For a Christian perspective on your self-worth, read:

- Matthew 10:29–31
- Matthew 12:11–12
- Luke 12:24

PSALM 93

THE LORD
REIGNS, HE IS
ROBED IN MAJESTY;
THE LORD IS
ROBED IN MAJESTY
AND ARMED WITH
STRENGTH; INDEED,
THE WORLD IS
ESTABLISHED, FIRM
AND SECURE.

—PSALM 93:1

A SONG OF PROPHECY

Psalm 93 is written by yet another author—Moses, the man who oversaw the creation of the nation of Israel and brought us God's Word. Just before his death, Moses wrote a song that describes—in poetic and cryptic terms—the entire history of the world that will unfold after his death until the end of time. It is recorded in the book of Deuteronomy, Chapter 32. These were among the last words that the great prophet ever uttered. Not surprisingly, they bear resemblance to his words in our psalm.

Moses ended his song this way: "*Rejoice, you nations, with his people, for he will avenge the blood of his servants; he will take vengeance on his enemies and make atonement for his land and people*" (Deuteronomy 32:43). Moses was speaking of a time when God will fight a war on behalf of His people, and it will be so obvious that He is the one leading the fight that it will cause rejoicing among the nations. This will be an event so spectacular that it will leave no doubt in anyone's mind that there is a Creator and that He

alone runs the world. God will be recognized as King and His Kingdom will be the entire earth.

Psalm 93 encompasses the very same theme. In the opening verse we are told, "*The LORD reigns, he is robed in majesty*" (v. 1). In verse 3, the psalmist described a raging and violent sea. Tradition teaches that this sea represents our enemies. But even the mightiest enemies were vanquished before the Lord who is "*mightier than the thunder of the great waters, mightier than the breakers of the sea*" (v. 4). The psalm concludes, "*holiness adorns your house for endless days*" (v. 5). Finally, God's Temple will be rebuilt, and He will reign as King for all of eternity.

Psalm 93 is both Friday's *Song of the Day* and part of the Sabbath day prayers. On the first Friday of the world, Adam and Eve, the first humans, were created. With their creation, it was possible for God to be recognized as King because now there were subjects. It was also impossible for humans to deny their Creator because they had just experienced their own creation. Every Friday, we attempt to return to such clarity by reading this psalm.

When we read the psalm again on the Sabbath, it has another meaning. Friday is the transition between the rest of the week and the Sabbath. It represents the transition time between history as we know it and the messianic era. During that time, God will perform great miracles in defense of His people and the whole world will recognize His sovereignty. This will pave the way for the Sabbath-like messianic era, when God will rule over a kingdom filled with tranquility, peace, holiness, and service to Him.

A CHRISTIAN SONG

God, the Lord, a King Remaineth

BASED ON PSALM 93

God, our Lord,
  a King remaineth,

Robed in His own
  glorious light;

God hath robed Him,
  and He reigneth;

He hath girded Him
  with might.

Alleluia! Alleluia!

God is King in depth
  and height!

—JOHN KEBLE (1792–1866)

Psalm 93

YOUR THRONE WAS ESTABLISHED LONG AGO; YOU ARE FROM ALL ETERNITY.

—PSALM 93:2

From Beyond This World

The Sages connect the second verse of Psalm 93 to the famous verse in Exodus which describes the aftermath of the parting of the Red Sea, *"Then Moses and the Israelites sang this song to the LORD"* (Exodus 15:1). The connecting link, they say, is the little word *ahz*. The same word is used in both verses and is the key to understanding both passages.

Judaism has a system in which every letter has a numerical value. Using this system, the word *ahz* equals the number eight. In Judaism, eight represents eternity. In fact, if you turn "8" on its side, you get the symbol for infinity.

Infinity is beyond time and beyond nature. It is the realm of the miraculous. Both passages are speaking about supernatural events. Exodus speaks about the beginning of the nation of Israel, while the psalm speaks about the End Times. In both cases, God performs miracles that are beyond nature and above reality.

After witnessing God's awesome wonders, Moses and the Israelites sang. However, an exact translation of the Hebrew gives a different meaning. The literal translations reads: "Then Moses and the Israelites will sing." While we understand the verse to be talking about the past, it is literally speaking about the future. This teaches us that just as miracles led to rejoicing with song in the past, they will have the same effect in the future. The miracles described in Psalm 93 will lead to the singing described in the book of Exodus.

What's the connection between miracles and singing?

DEVOTION

Just as miracles are from beyond our world, so is song. A friend of mine once said, "Good music takes us back to places we used to be, but great music takes us to places that we've never been." Music can move us beyond the physical world and give us a taste of infinity.

Since the inception of the nation of Israel, music has played a central role. Songs were sung after great victories, and with King David, music and song became a regular means of worship. Prophets used music as a way of getting into a prophetic state, and priests made music to enhance the Temple experience. Music has always gone hand-in-hand with transcending reality, and that explains why, when we experience the supernatural—whether in ancient times or times yet to come—the most natural response is to sing.

Friends, if miracles lead to singing, then singing can bring us to miracles. When we sing to the Lord, we reach beyond this world and we invite the miraculous into our lives. As the world stands at a dangerous crossroads, we must reach into the heavens with the power of our song. We may not be able to talk our way out of this mess, but we can sing our way to an entirely new reality—one that is beyond this world.

GOING DEEPER FOR CHRISTIANS

For a Christian perspective on songs and singing, read:

- 1 Corinthians 14:15

- Ephesians 5:15–19

- Colossians 3:16

- James 5:13

PSALM 94

THE LORD IS
A GOD WHO
AVENGES. O GOD
WHO AVENGES,
SHINE FORTH.
RISE UP, JUDGE
OF THE EARTH;
PAY BACK TO THE
PROUD WHAT
THEY DESERVE.

—PSALM 94:1–2

A SONG OF TRIUMPH

Psalm 94 is one of 11 psalms written by Moses. While in the previous psalm (93), Moses talked about God's ultimate dominion over the world, in this psalm, he spells out what that will mean exactly. The triumph of God over His enemies will mean the victory of good over evil. At the end of time, goodness will reign.

The Sages teach that the redemption at the end of time will mirror the original redemption—the exodus from Egypt. So while Psalm 94 is a prophecy about future events, it also mirrors the events that unfolded in Moses' lifetime. When Moses writes about evil oppressing the innocent and of the murder of the defenseless, we are reminded of the evil Egyptians who enslaved and killed the defenseless children of Israel.

In this psalm, Moses asked, "*How long will the wicked be jubilant?*" (v. 3) just as he asked God, "*Why, LORD, why have you brought trouble on this people?*" (Exodus 5:22). But in the end, Moses wrote, "*He will repay them for their sins and destroy*

them for their wickedness" (v. 23). The end of all evildoers will be the same as the Egyptians who were washed away by the sea.

Psalm 94 was chosen to be the *Song of the Day* for Wednesday, the fourth day of Creation. On that day, God created the sun, moon, and stars. These great luminaries represent the gifts that God bestows upon humanity. However they also represent how we can misuse those gifts. In a great twist of irony, the luminaries in the sky were used against the One who created them. The original form of idol worship was the worship of the lights in the sky.

Jewish tradition teaches that initially, every human being recognized God as Creator and ruler of the world. They saw the sun, moon, and stars as God's great servants. Through them, God would send blessings to the world. Just as one would honor a king's closest advisors, they thought it was befitting to honor God's luminaries. Eventually, however, they gave more and more honor to God's servants and less attention to God Himself. The transition was complete when they paid all tribute to the heavenly spheres and none to God. They could only see the intermediaries that delivered blessings, and they forgot entirely about the source of them all.

All evil comes from forgetting the Lord. For anyone who knows that God is the source of all blessings and ruler of the earth, it is foolish to work against Him. But fools are exactly what Moses calls the evil ones: "*You fools, when will you become wise?*" (v. 8). Wise up, says Moses. Remember who is in charge. Those who do evil make a grave mistake—one for which they will pay dearly.

When we read Psalm 94 in the middle of every week, we recognize that God is the source of blessings, and we remember to use His gifts wisely.

A CHRISTIAN SONG

Rock of Ages
BASED ON PSALM 94:22

Rock of Ages, cleft for me,

Let me hide myself
   in Thee;

Let the water and
   the blood,

From Thy wounded
   side which flowed,

Be of sin the double cure,

Save from wrath and
   make me pure.

—AUGUSTUS TOPLADY
(1740–1778)

Psalm 94

HOW LONG, LORD,

WILL THE WICKED,

HOW LONG WILL

THE WICKED

BE JUBILANT?

—PSALM 94:3

Why Do the Wicked Prosper?

Psalm 94 is about justice and an affirmation that justice will prevail. But hidden in the psalm is a question about God's judgment. The psalmist wrote, *"How long will the wicked be jubilant?"* How can You let the wicked prosper while the righteous suffer? Where's the justice? That's what Moses wanted to know. We know from the Bible that this is a conversation Moses and God already had.

Jewish tradition teaches that when Moses said to God, *"Show me your glory"* (Exodus 33:18), he was asking God to explain the way that He runs the world. Moses wanted to understand how a world that looks so unfair could possibly be just. Here is God's answer to Moses: *"I will have mercy on whom I will have mercy, and I will have compassion on whom I will have compassion. But . . . you cannot see my face, for no one may see me and live"* (Exodus 33:19–20).

How are we to understand this cryptic answer?

The Sages explain God's words this way: I will have mercy on the people that I see deserving of mercy. You may not think that they deserve it, but I do. God's first point is that human beings do not have the capacity to decide who is deserving and who is undeserving. The holiest-looking person may be hiding his corruption, while a person whom we perceive as lowly may be a humble servant of God.

Second, God says, in essence, I will have compassion—what I know to be true compassion—on those who are deserving. What you perceive as cruelty is what I know to be compassion. Often, what looks like a terrible curse turns out to be the greatest blessing. On the other hand, what we may think is compassion can really be a punishment. God may give the wicked all their blessings at once in order that they enjoy no goodness in the future. Sometimes it's only in the afterlife that the wicked receive punishment for their sins.

Finally, God says, you cannot see my face and live. A few verses later He explains, "*You will see my back; but my face must not be seen*" (Exodus 33:23). God is telling Moses, and all of us, that when we are staring life in the face, we won't be able to understand how it is just. But in retrospect—when we look back on history—we can begin to understand God's plan.

All three ideas come down to the same three words: We don't know. We are not capable of understanding God's ways. But we are capable of having faith in them. Psalm 94 gives us strength to believe in God's justice even when injustice is all that we can see.

The psalm ends with this assurance: "*He will repay them for their sins and destroy them for their wickedness*" (v.23). Make no mistake about it—in the end, justice will be served.

GOING DEEPER FOR CHRISTIANS

For a Christian perspective on understanding God's wisdom, read:

- Romans 11:33–34

- 1 Corinthians 2:10–16

PSALM 95

COME, LET US

SING FOR JOY TO

THE LORD; LET US

SHOUT ALOUD TO

THE ROCK OF

OUR SALVATION.

LET US COME

BEFORE HIM WITH

THANKSGIVING

AND EXTOL HIM

WITH MUSIC

AND SONG.

—PSALM 95:1–2

A SONG OF JOY

Psalm 95 is yet another psalm written by Moses. Like earlier psalms by Moses, this also describes the messianic era. At the same time, it contains references to Moses' lifetime.

This psalm is an invitation to sing to the Lord: "*Come, let us sing for joy to the LORD; let us shout aloud to the Rock of our salvation*" (v. 1). We are reminded of the song that Moses and the Israelites sang just after they experienced the parting of the Red Sea. Later in the psalm, we find references to Massah and Meribah. There, the children of Israel doubted that God could provide water for them, so God had Moses bring forth water from a rock. The psalm ends with a reminder of the fate of that faithless generation who Moses led out of Egypt. Since they lacked faith in God, they were not allowed to enter the Promised Land.

In spite of the psalm's somber ending, Psalm 95 is overflowing with joy, "*Let us come before him with thanksgiving and extol him with music and song*" (v. 2); "*Come, let us bow down in worship, let us kneel before the* LORD *our Maker*" (v. 6). It's a vision of the messianic era when all humanity will praise the Lord. In that thrilling time, there will be unity between people and between God and His Creation.

Psalm 95 has the privilege of beginning the Friday night prayer service known as *Receiving the Sabbath*. The Sabbath is a day of unity—a day in which we grow closer to the people around us and to our Creator. It is a day of joy and praise; a day to focus on our blessings. We leave our hectic lives behind us and celebrate a day of tranquility.

Since it isn't easy to turn off the static of our lives and tune in to the spirit of the Sabbath, it became traditional to prepare for this holy day. There are two types of preparations that must be made. We prepare physically by cooking a festive meal, making our homes clean and beautiful, and dressing in our finest clothing. We prepare spiritually by taking the time to adopt the proper state of mind. The rabbis created the *Receiving the Sabbath* service as a special observance for this purpose. The service is full of psalms that help us focus our minds by reaching into our souls.

The mystical masters who lived in the holy city of Safed in northern Israel during the 16th century took this practice one step further. They understood the first verse of our psalm, "*Come, let us sing for joy to the* LORD . . .*" (v. 1), as an invitation to go somewhere. They began the practice of leaving the city and going out to the fields and forests in order to greet the Sabbath. There, they could more easily disconnect from everyday life and attach themselves to the Lord. Among the trees and birds, they would sing this psalm and receive the holy Sabbath.

A CHRISTIAN SONG

Come, Christians, Join to Sing

BASED ON PSALM 95:1

Come, Christians,
*   join to sing*

Alleluia! Amen!

Loud praise to
*   Christ our King;*

Alleluia! Amen!

Let all, with heart
*   and voice,*

Before His throne rejoice;

Praise is His
*   gracious choice.*

Alleluia! Amen!

—CHRISTIAN H. BATEMAN
(1813–1889)

Psalm 95

FOR HE IS
OUR GOD AND
WE ARE THE
PEOPLE OF HIS
PASTURE, THE
FLOCK UNDER
HIS CARE.

—PSALM 95:7

Inspiration and Action

Although most of Psalm 95 is full of joy, we can't ignore the last third of the psalm which shifts dramatically in tone. We begin with jubilant calls to praise the Lord, but end with a harsh admonishment reminding us of the ill fate of those who fail to obey God. Why did the psalmist place these two, very different ideas in the same psalm?

The answer can be found in verse 7. It is the link that joins the two seemingly disparate parts: "*For he is our God and we are the people of his pasture, the flock under his care.*" This verse is both the reason for our joy and a call for obedience. On one hand, there is the beautiful thought of being one of God's sheep. He guides and cares for us as any good shepherd would. But at the same time, we are reminded that a shepherd can only take care of sheep that follow him. He can't help those who refuse to follow. A shepherd is only as effective as his sheep are obedient.

Moses had seen what happens to sheep who fail to follow. He saw the exuberance of the Israelites after God performed miracles for them. They were on an amazing spiritual high. But then, just as quickly as they soared, they fell to the ground. They repeatedly lost their faith during their wanderings in the desert and refused to follow God into the Promised Land. Moses' experience had taught him that it's not enough to talk the talk—or in their case, to sing the song; one must also walk the walk.

Psalm 95 is not two separate ideas—it is two parts of one whole. The first part deals with inspiration; the second, with action. Service

DEVOTION

to God is incomplete without both. Action without feeling is dry, but feelings of inspiration are meaningless when action doesn't follow.

I heard the following story from a friend, Avi, who is a very busy man. His father was coming to visit and asked Avi to pick him up from the airport, right in the middle of rush hour. "Dad, I love you, but I just can't get away for that long. I'll send a car service," Avi offered. But the father wanted his son to greet him at the airport and insisted that Avi come. "Dad, I love you so much. But I just can't do it," Avi tried again. "Just come," the father said. "I love you, but I can't," came Avi's refrain. Finally the father said, "Stop loving me so much and just pick me up from the airport." And he hung up the phone. Feelings don't mean much if it we don't act on them.

The beginning of Psalm 95 is all about feelings of inspiration, but in the end, we are reminded to follow up with our deeds. Only both make our service to God whole.

This psalm begs the question: What actions can you take to express your love for God?

GOING DEEPER FOR CHRISTIANS

For a Christian perspective on faith and action, read:

- Matthew 7:17–20

- Matthew 25:35–36

- James 2:14–18

- 1 John 3:18–19

PSALM 100

ENTER HIS

GATES WITH

THANKSGIVING

AND HIS COURTS

WITH PRAISE;

GIVE THANKS

TO HIM AND

PRAISE HIS NAME.

—PSALM 100:4

A SONG FOR THANKSGIVING

The introduction to Psalm 100 tells us exactly what it was intended for: "*A psalm. For giving grateful praise.*" This psalm was composed for the purpose of giving thanks to the Lord for the many blessings that He bestows upon us. More specifically, this psalm was intended for use in the Temple.

There was a special sacrifice designated for expressing gratitude known as the "thanksgiving offering." It was traditionally offered after a person experienced one of four situations: release from imprisonment; healing from severe illness; crossing the sea; or travelling across a desert. After a person safely endured one of these life-threatening situations, he or she would go to the Temple and thank God for His protection. As an offering was brought, Psalm 100 would be recited.

The psalmist wrote, "*Enter his gates with thanksgiving and his courts with praise; give thanks to him and praise his name*" (v. 4). The gates in the psalm refer to the Temple gates and the courtyard is the place where sacrifices were made. One of the purposes of the Temple was to serve as a place where people could connect to God by recognizing all He has given them. The Temple was a place of awe, but as this psalm tells us, it was also a place of rejoicing. Sometimes people would go to atone for their sins, but other times it would be a place to celebrate their blessings.

The thanksgiving offering was an especially festive event. It consisted of animal offerings as well as different kinds of bread that were to be eaten as part of the celebration. One of the unique laws regarding the offering was that it had to be eaten by the end of the night. This ensured that the person hosting the feast would invite friends and family to join the festivities. One person couldn't possibly eat it all! This made the feast especially joyous and also served as a greater tribute to God. His goodness would be known to many and gratitude would be expressed by all.

Psalm 100 has become part of our daily prayer service. Since we experience miracles every single day—even if we don't even realize it—the Sages felt that it was appropriate to express our gratitude with this psalm. It is recited in a section of the service known as *Verses of Praise*. The goal of this portion of the service is to put the worshiper in the proper state of mind. As we recite this psalm, we recognize that God is the source of all blessings and we thank Him for all that He has given us. It is in the context of gratitude that we approach God with our new requests.

A CHRISTIAN SONG

The Old Hundredth

BASED ON PSALM 100

*All people that
    on earth do dwell,*

*sing to the Lord
    with cheerful voice.*

*Him serve with mirth,
    his praise forthtell;*

*come ye before him
    and rejoice.*

—WILLIAM KETHE
(16TH CENTURY)

Psalm 100

WORSHIP THE

LORD WITH

GLADNESS;

COME BEFORE

HIM WITH

JOYFUL SONGS.

—PSALM 100:2

A Happy State of Mind

The psalmist tells us to *"Worship the LORD with gladness."* But can we really be told how to feel?

In the book of Deuteronomy, God makes a similar demand. He describes the blessings that will rain down on us when we follow His commands. Then, He enumerates the horrible curses that will plague us when our behavior is lacking.

Why do we deserve to be cursed instead of blessed? *"Because you did not serve the LORD your God joyfully and gladly . . ."* (Deuteronomy 28:47). Curses come upon us when we don't serve God with joy. Isn't that unfair? Sometimes life is extremely difficult. How can God fault us for feeling sad?

A closer reading of the rest of the verse from Deuteronomy provides the answer, *"Because you did not serve the LORD your God joyfully and gladly in the time of prosperity."* The problem isn't that we feel down in times of trouble. The issue is that we aren't joyful and grateful in times of plenty. No one can blame us for being sad sometimes. But there are times in our lives when, if we aren't full of joy, there is something seriously wrong. When we fail to recognize our blessings, we simply don't deserve them.

Comedian Louis C.K. has a bit called "Everything's Amazing, and Nobody is Happy," in which he talks about airplane travel. As he explains, many people describe their experience flying as the worst day of their lives. But, he says, what happened after waiting on the runway for 40 minutes or more before finally taking off?

DEVOTION

"Did you fly in the air like a bird? Did you partake in the miracle of human flight? It's amazing! Everybody on every flight should be constantly screaming, 'Oh my God!!! This is amazing!!!' You are sitting in a chair in the sky! But then we complain, 'the seat doesn't go back a lot.'"

He continues, "People complain about flight delays. But, New York to California used to take years! Do you know what that means? On the way, people would be born and people would die. You would be an entirely different group when you got there! Now, you watch a movie and go to the bathroom and you're home!"

Indeed, we are living in truly amazing times. But what do we focus on? That we can fly in the sky, or that our chair doesn't recline as much as we would like it to? In Hebrew, the word for "happy" is spelled with the same exact letters as the word for "thought." In other words, our thoughts control our happiness. And while we may not be able to help how we feel, we can help what we think about.

Friends, life gives us enough to be sad about. Let's not pass up even one chance to be happy. Let us celebrate every miracle and feel joy at every blessing. Let us give thanks to God and serve Him with joy, and yes, gladness. We have so much to be thankful for, and with gratitude, we will receive even more.

GOING DEEPER FOR CHRISTIANS

For a Christian perspective on thanksgiving, read:

- Luke 9:16
- Romans 1:21
- Ephesians 5:3–5
- Philippians 4:6
- 1 Thessalonians 5:16–18
- 1 Timothy 2:1
- Revelation 11:16–17

PSALM 103

PRAISE THE LORD,
MY SOUL, AND
FORGET NOT ALL
HIS BENEFITS.

—PSALM 103:2

A SONG OF PRAISE

Psalm 103 is a distinct call to praise: "*Praise the LORD, my soul, and forget not all his benefits*" (v. 2). The psalmist continues, thanking God for the many gifts that He bestows upon His children, emphasizing the great gift of forgiveness. The psalm concludes the same way it began: "*Praise the LORD, all his works everywhere in his dominion. Praise the LORD, my soul*" (v. 22). The psalmist urges every part of Creation to join him in praising the Creator.

King David is legendary for praising God throughout every part of his life. The Sages teach that he was composing psalms before he was even born! Whether or not we are to take that claim literally, the Sages were making a point: the very essence of David's soul was to praise God. In Psalm 103, every time that David writes "*Praise the LORD, my soul*," it corresponds with a milestone in his early life.

For example, the first verse in Psalm 103 relates to the time when David was in his mother's womb, "*Praise the LORD, my soul; all my inmost being, praise his holy name*" (v. 1). The "inmost being" in this verse is David, deep inside his mother's being. Even before his birth, David had a song on his lips.

The next major event in David's life was his birth. As he entered this world and looked up at the stars in the sky, his soul was stirred and he sang, "*Praise the LORD, you his angels, you mighty ones who do his bidding, who obey his word. Praise the LORD, all his heavenly hosts . . .*" (vv. 20–21). David saw the angels and stars and appreciated the greatness of God.

As the infant David received the nourishment of his mother's milk, he sang, "*Praise the LORD, my soul, and forget not all his benefits*" (v. 2). David understood that God was providing for him from the very beginning, and he appreciated God's love.

Again, David probably didn't utter any of these words as a baby. Maybe he thought them or maybe he composed them later in life. But the message is clear: Even before any of us are born, there is reason enough to praise God. The first few moments of life are cause for joyful singing. How much more so should we sing to the Lord for all the years that we have already been given on this earth!

The first line of Psalm 103 ends one of the special prayers said on the Sabbath. The prayer, which begins "The soul of every being will praise Your Name," bears a strong resemblance to Psalm 103. It is said on the Sabbath because it is on the day of rest that, like David, we can step back and appreciate the many blessings that we receive from God every single day of our lives.

A CHRISTIAN SONG

Joyful, Joyful, We Adore Thee

BASED ON PSALM 103:22

Joyful, joyful,
* we adore You,*

God of glory, Lord of love;

Hearts unfold like
* flow'rs before You,*

Op'ning to the sun above.

Melt the clouds
* of sin and sadness;*

Drive the dark
* of doubt away;*

Giver of immortal
* gladness,*

Fill us with
* the light of day!*

—HENRY VAN DYKE
(1852–1933)

Psalm 103

PRAISE THE LORD,

MY SOUL; ALL MY

INMOST BEING,

PRAISE HIS

HOLY NAME.

—PSALM 103:1

Body and Soul

The psalmist encourages us to praise the Lord with our entire being, *"all my inmost being, praise his holy name."* Praise is something that comes from our hearts and goes out through our mouths. So how do we involve our whole body in praising God?

In a word, the answer is in our actions. We praise God with our whole being when we turn the gratitude in our hearts into the actions of our bodies. We thank God for all that He has given us and then we dedicate our entire being to His service.

A while back, a friend was looking for domestic help in her house, and the person that she hired seemed different from the others she had hired previously. For starters, this woman drove a very nice car. As my friend got to know her better, she learned that this woman was well-educated, married to a successful doctor, and that she enjoyed a very nice life together with her family.

One day, my friend felt close enough to the woman to ask the question that she had been burning to ask from the first day: "Why are you working for me? You don't seem to need the money!" The woman laughed and then explained, "The money isn't for me. It's for my church. You see, the church is in desperate need of funding. So my friends and I decided to do something to help. We couldn't give any more money than we already had given, so those of us who are

DEVOTION

housewives decided to go to work. Every penny that you are paying me is going to my church."

The woman who worked for my friend knew how to praise the Lord with every part of her body. As she washed the dishes, she served the Lord. As she polished the silver, she served the Lord. As she got down on her hands and knees to scrub floors and clean toilets, she served the Lord. She didn't just make the house sparkle; she added light to the world.

We already know how to praise the Lord with our mouths. There is no shortage of hymns or psalms in which to do so. But how can you praise the Lord with your whole being?

Consider this: Use your eyes to read God's Word. Use your ears to listen to a friend. Use your nose to smell the food that you are eating and use your mouth to thank God for sustenance. Use your heart to feel compassion for someone who is hurting, and use your arms to give them a big, warm hug. Use your hands to help and to heal and your legs to take you on missions of kindness. Every part of your being is a tool for praising the Lord.

Let us echo the psalmist and praise God with all of our being—body and soul.

GOING DEEPER FOR CHRISTIANS

For a Christian perspective on giving praise, read:

- Romans 15:7–12
- 2 Corinthians 1:3
- Ephesians 1:3
- Hebrews 13:15
- 1 Peter 2:9

PSALM 114

WHEN ISRAEL
CAME OUT OF
EGYPT, JACOB
FROM A PEOPLE
OF FOREIGN
TONGUE, JUDAH
BECAME GOD'S
SANCTUARY,
ISRAEL HIS
DOMINION.

—PSALM 114:1–2

A SONG OF GENERATIONS

Psalm 114 is part of a group of six psalms that were first sung after the Israelites crossed the Red Sea. It is a psalm of praise describing and celebrating the amazing events that followed the exodus from Egypt in very vivid word pictures. It describes the sea *"fleeing,"* the Jordan *"retreating,"* and mountains *"leaping like rams."*

And indeed, that is exactly what happened. The sea fled when it parted in order to allow the Israelites to safely escape their Egyptian enemies. The waters of the Jordan River retreated when the Israelites crossed to the Promised Land. And the mountains shook when God descended on Mount Sinai in order to give Moses the Ten Commandments and the *Torah*. The psalm ends with a reference to a hard rock turning into springs of water, which occurred when Moses struck

a rock and brought forth water in the desert.

In its eight short verses, Psalm 114 recounts the many miracles that brought about the birth of the nation of Israel!

Tradition teaches that this psalm, along with the other five in its group, was passed down from generation to generation long before David compiled them in the book of Psalms, and then were passed on to future generations long after David. They were recited by Joshua after he defeated the kings of Canaan; Deborah and Barak after they defeated Sisera; Hezekiah after he defeated Sennacherib; and Mordecai and Esther after they defeated Haman.

These psalms have accompanied every major event where God came to the aid of His children, just as He did when He took them out of Egypt. They are an expression of gratitude to the Lord and a reminder of what is possible when He is on our side.

The *Talmud* asks why Psalms 113–118 were chosen as the script for giving praise long after the Israelites left Egypt. It explains that this group of psalms contains five fundamental and timeless themes in the Jewish faith: the exodus; the parting of the Red Sea; the giving of the *Torah* at Mount Sinai; the future resurrection of the dead; and the coming of the Messiah. These five elements are so essential to our belief in God's sovereignty that they are remembered every time we see His hand in action.

The tradition of reciting this group of psalms during times of celebration is continued today. They form a service known as *Hallel*, which literally means "praise," and is recited on every Jewish holiday and every new moon. It is inserted into the morning prayer service and is sung with great joy. It is also a central part of the Passover *seder*. While the *seder* begins with the telling of the exodus story, it ends with the jubilant singing of *Hallel*.

The words composed by the Israelites thousands of years ago are echoed throughout the year today. We are continuing the journey that they began when they left Egypt, and we will travel on until we enter the messianic era, repeating the words of *Hallel* along the way.

A CHRISTIAN SONG

Go Down, Moses

BASED ON PSALM 114:1

*When Israel was
   in Egypt's land,*

Let my people go,

*oppressed so hard
   they could not stand,*

Let my people go.

Refrain:

*Go down, Moses, way
   down in Egypt's land,*

*tell old Pharaoh:
   Let my people go.*

—Anonymous; African-
American Spiritual

Psalm 114

THE SEA LOOKED

AND FLED,

THE JORDAN

TURNED BACK

—PSALM 114:3

ALWAYS LOOKING

In Psalm 114 we read about the exodus from Egypt. The psalmist reveals that when the Israelites approached the Red Sea it "*looked and fled.*" What did the sea look at that made it leave?

Jewish tradition teaches that the sea saw the bones of Joseph, the son of Jacob, who had requested that the Israelites take his remains with them when they left Egypt. Something about the bones of Joseph caused the sea to react. What? For the answer, we turn to Joseph's moment of triumph.

Joseph's greatest achievement was not becoming the viceroy of Egypt. It wasn't even his willingness to help out his brothers even though they hadn't exactly treated him so nicely. Joseph's greatest moment came when he refused the advances of the wife of his master.

After being sold into slavery in Egypt, Joseph found himself working in the home of Potiphar. Potiphar's wife took a liking to him and tried daily to ensnare Joseph in sin. Against his grain, Joseph was able to refuse her offers, "*'How then could I do such a wicked thing and sin against God?' And though she spoke to Joseph day after day, he refused to go to bed with her or even be with her*" (Genesis 39:9–10). Joseph fought against his natural desires, and he won.

Such self-mastery is an achievement like no other. The Sages teach that when the sea saw the remains of Joseph, it said, "If Joseph can go against his nature, I can go against my nature, too." And it split.

The sea mastered its natural tendency because it saw Joseph. But where did Joseph get his strength from? Whom did Joseph see?

DEVOTION

The *Talmud* gives us a window into Joseph's mind just before he ran away from Potiphar's wife. Joseph was about to succumb to sin when he saw a vision of his father, Jacob. Seeing Jacob gave him the strength to persevere. The sea's inspiration was Joseph, but Joseph's inspiration was his saintly father.

A poem titled, "When You Thought I Wasn't Looking," describes all the great life lessons that the author learned from her mother when the mother didn't notice. For example, when the mother fed a stray cat, the child learned to care for all living things. When the mother hung the child's painting on the refrigerator, the child learned that she mattered. The poem ends by saying, "When you thought I wasn't looking, I looked." The author thanked her mother for all that she taught her without even knowing it.

Friends, let us remember that the children are always looking. They are watching and learning from our every move. Are we kind and caring? Are we honest and just? How do we act when we become angry? Children learn best by modeling the behavior of the adults around them. This is our greatest opportunity and our grave responsibility.

GOING DEEPER FOR CHRISTIANS

For a Christian perspective on teaching the next generation, read:

- Matthew 28:19–20
- Ephesians 6:4
- Colossians 3:21
- 1 Timothy 1:18–19

PSALM 121

I LIFT UP MY
EYES TO THE
MOUNTAINS—
WHERE DOES
MY HELP COME
FROM? MY HELP
COMES FROM
THE LORD, THE
MAKER OF HEAVEN
AND EARTH.

—PSALM 121:1–2

A SONG FOR THE JOURNEY

There are 15 psalms—Psalms 120–134—that are called *Songs of Ascent*. How did they get their name and what is their purpose? It's a bit of a mystery, but most commentators agree that whatever the origin of these psalms, they all served a similar function when the Temple stood. These were the psalms sung by the priests as they ascended the steps of the house of the Lord.

The courtyard outside the Temple was divided into two main sections. Connecting the two sections were fifteen stairs, and it was the job of a group of priests to sing holy songs in order to enhance the Temple experience. They would sing these 15 psalms as they ascended the stairs. On each stair they would pause and sing one psalm. The worshipers in the Temple could both hear and visualize the ascension to the Lord.

While all the *Songs of Ascent* are uplifting in nature (another explanation as to how they got their name), Psalm 121 begins with the imagery of literally looking up: "*I lift up my eyes to the mountains—where does my help come from?*" (v. 1). The psalmist was looking up to find the source of his salvation, recognizing that his help comes from God above, "*My help comes from the Lord, the Maker of heaven and earth*" (v. 2).

The Sages teach that the inspiration for this psalm came from the book of Genesis when Jacob had to leave his home in order to escape his brother Esau. On that perilous journey, Jacob had a dream in which he encountered God. God promised Jacob that everything would work out and reassured Jacob with the following words, "*I am with you and will watch over you wherever you go, and I will bring you back to this land . . .*" (Genesis 28:15). Psalm 121 ends with very similar words, "*the Lord will watch over your coming and going both now and forevermore*" (v. 8).

Appropriately, it has become customary to recite Psalm 121 before beginning any long or dangerous journey. Just as God watched and protected Jacob, we pray that He will provide us with the same closeness and protection.

This psalm is also recited when going through any difficult time. Anything from illness to danger in the State of Israel moves us to ask God for special protection. The words of this psalm give expression to our cry for help and give us comfort that our salvation will come. In some communities, Psalm 121 is recited every night. In the dark times of our lives, this psalm is a light shining upward. It points to the heavens, reminding us that we are never alone.

A CHRISTIAN SONG

Unto the Hills

BASED ON PSALM 121

*Unto the hills around
    do I lift up*

my longing eyes:

*O whence for me shall
    my salvation come,*

from whence arise?

*From God the Lord doth
    come my certain aid,*

*from God the Lord
    who heaven and earth
    hath made.*

—John Douglas
Southerland Campbell
(1845–1914)

Psalm 121

THE LORD WILL
KEEP YOU FROM
ALL HARM—
HE WILL WATCH
OVER YOUR LIFE.

—PSALM 121:7

Plus One

The Sages teach that Psalm 121 is a conversation between a father and son. It takes place just as the son is about to begin a long journey and the father is seeing him off. As they stand at the start of the road, they gaze at the mountains in the distance. Their conversation goes something like this:

Son: *As I look at these mountains I wonder who will help me on the long road ahead. But I realize that God, who created heaven and earth, can help me through anything.*

Father: *God won't let your foot slip for even a moment; He is always watching you.*

Son: *Indeed, God is always alert and watching; He doesn't doze off or sleep.*

Father: *God watches over you and is so close, like shade shielding you from the sun. May the Lord protect you now and forever.*

At first glance it seems that the father and son are just repeating the same idea throughout the entire conversation—God watches over us. But the truth is that when the father first speaks, he introduces his son to a totally different concept.

The son says that he knows that God can help him because God is in charge of all the earth. But the father says that God isn't just the Creator; He is also the Sustainer. God didn't just create the world and then retreat to heaven until someone is in dire need of His help. God sticks around and is involved in every

DEVOTION

minute detail of life. To the son, God is the One Who created everything and lives in the sky. But the father explains that God is by our side with every single step that we take here on earth.

Uri Zohar is a famous Israeli actor who left his career in order to immerse himself in his newfound passion for the Bible and service to God. When he was leaving the life of comic entertainment, his friends begged him for one last parting joke. This was it:

Two religious guys were riding on a motorcycle when they were noticed by a secular policeman. The policeman, who had it out for religious people, stalked them and waited for them to break any rule so that he could give them a ticket. But the two made no mistakes! They stopped at every stop sign and stayed well beneath the speed limit. In utter frustration, the policeman pulled the pair over and asked, "How do you manage to drive so perfectly?" They answered, "How could we possibly mess up? God is with us!" The officer responded, "Aha! Now I've got you! Having three on a motorcycle is against the law."

Wherever we go and whomever we are with, we are always plus one more. The psalmist puts it this way: "*The Lord will keep you from all harm—he will watch over your life.*" Like a shield that completely surrounds us, God is present at every moment in our lives.

GOING DEEPER FOR CHRISTIANS

For a Christian perspective on God's care for you, read:

- Matthew 28:20
- Luke 12:6–7
- Romans 16:25
- 2 Corinthians 1:4
- Jude 24–25

PSALM 122

I REJOICED
WITH THOSE
WHO SAID TO
ME, 'LET US GO
TO THE HOUSE
OF THE LORD.'
OUR FEET ARE
STANDING IN
YOUR GATES,
JERUSALEM.

—PSALM 122:1–2

A SONG FOR GOD'S HOUSE

Psalm 122 is one of the *Songs of Ascent* and is an uplifting song about the city of Jerusalem. Jerusalem is the site of the "*house of the LORD*" (v. 1), and "*where the tribes go up . . . to praise the name of the LORD*" (v. 4). No place was more joyful than Jerusalem when pilgrims would visit on holidays or beseech God in the Temple. The psalm ends

Israeli paratroopers after capturing Western Wall in 1967
(Photo courtesy of the Israeli Government Press Office)

with King David asking us to "*Pray for the peace of Jerusalem*" (v. 6) and for those who love her. Only when Jerusalem is safe and secure can she be the source of gladness as God intended.

This psalm was originally written for the time period in which King David was living. After David captured the city of Jerusalem, he wanted nothing more than to build God's Temple. But God said, "*You are not to build a house for my Name, because you have shed much blood on the earth*" (1 Chronicles 22:8). David's job was to fight God's battles, but at the same time, it made him unfit to build the house of God. The Temple had to be built by a man of peace. Solomon, David's son, would fulfill his father's dream.

The people in David's kingdom knew that the Temple would only be constructed after his death. So when they longed for the Temple, they inadvertently were wishing for their king's demise. But David wrote, "*I rejoiced with those who said to me, 'Let us go to the house of the LORD*'" (v. 1). David was humble—he joined the people in their longing to build God's Temple. He joyfully anticipated the new era, even though it meant the end of his own lifetime. He wrote this psalm as an expression of his longing for the time when the Temple would be built and Jerusalem would enjoy peace. He wouldn't live to see that day, but he yearned for it just the same.

History has come full circle as once again, this psalm takes the stage. Over two thousand years ago, the Jewish people lost sovereignty over Jerusalem when they were sent into exile. Jerusalem was out of Jewish control . . . until now. In 1967, Israel fought the Six-Day War and liberated Jerusalem. At the close of the war, the radio broadcast a message that was heard around the world: "The Temple Mount is in our hands!" After a moment of silence, the broadcaster recited Psalm 122: "*Our feet are standing in your gates, Jerusalem*" (v. 2). The two-thousand-year-old dream had come true.

Every year since 1967, Israel celebrates "Jerusalem Day" on the Hebrew date that it was liberated. As part of the celebrations, we recite this psalm. However, this psalm is appropriate on any day during these times. Once again, Jerusalem is in our possession, but we long for the day that we can rebuild the holy Temple and the city will be at peace.

A CHRISTIAN SONG

Jerusalem, My Happy Home
BASED ON 122:2

Jerusalem, my happy home,
Name ever dear to me,
When shall my labours
    have an end,
In joy and peace, with thee?
When shall these eyes
    thy heaven-built walls
And pearly gates behold?
Thy bulwarks, with
    salvation strong,
And streets of shining gold?

—ATTRIBUTED TO JOSEPH
BROMEHEAD (1747–1826)

Psalm 122

FOR THE SAKE
OF MY FAMILY
AND FRIENDS,
I WILL SAY, 'PEACE
BE WITHIN YOU.'
FOR THE SAKE OF
THE HOUSE OF THE
LORD OUR GOD,
I WILL SEEK YOUR
PROSPERITY.

—PSALM 122:8–9

Family First

There was once a poor family who was struggling to put food on the table. As a last resort, the father sent his two oldest sons out into the great big world in hopes that they could make enough money to support themselves and take a bit of the burden off his shoulders. One brother, Joseph, became extremely successful and eventually became the head of a large business. Jacob struggled for survival and just barely got by.

With time, the successful brother forgot his roots, his family, and the poverty he had come from. But Jacob never forgot who his family was and decided to turn to his wealthy brother for help. He traveled far to Joseph's town and office in order to ask for a job. But when he got there, he was told that Joseph was unavailable.

"Tell him that it's his brother who is waiting to see him," Jacob eagerly told the secretary. The woman went back to her boss and said, "The poor man waiting to see you claims that he is your brother. Should I let him through?" Joseph didn't have time for needy relatives. "I don't have a brother," came his cold reply.

Sometime later, both brothers received a letter informing them that their father was deathly ill. Both returned home to share the last precious moments with their father. After spending some time together, Joseph realized that his father had not spoken a single word to him or even acknowledged his presence. With tears dripping down his cheeks, he said, "Father, why are you ignoring me?" The father—who knew all

DEVOTION

about how his rich son had treated his other son—said, "You must be mistaken. How could I be your father? If Jacob is not your brother, I cannot possibly be your father, because Jacob is my son."

Psalm 122 ends with a prayer, first "*for the sake of my family and friends,*" and then "*for the sake of the house of the LORD.*" The Sages teach that the two requests are related. First, we wish the best for the people around us. We must see them as "*family and friends*" and treat them accordingly. Only then, can we pray for the house of the Lord and hope that we will see the day when God returns to His earthly dwelling place. Just like the father in the story, God says, "I can only be your father if you treat my children like your brothers." We must become a family if we want our heavenly Father to return.

When someone asks us for money, it's tempting to look the other way. But how can you ignore the poor woman before you if she is your sister? How can you watch the homeless man shiver when he is your brother? Next time you find yourself turning away from a plea for help, remember, if we want God to treat us like a father, then we have to treat His children like our family.

GOING DEEPER FOR CHRISTIANS

For a Christian perspective on God's family, read:

- Galatians 6:9–11
- Ephesians 2:19
- 1 Thessalonians 3:12
- 1 Thessalonians 4:9–10

PSALM 126

THOSE WHO GO

OUT WEEPING,

CARRYING SEED

TO SOW, WILL

RETURN WITH

SONGS OF JOY,

CARRYING SHEAVES

WITH THEM.

—PSALM 126:6

A SONG OF REDEMPTION

The first line of Psalm 126 indicates when it was written: "*When the LORD restored the fortunes of Zion . . .*" (v. 1). The destruction of the first Temple in 586 B.C.E. led to a 70-year period of exile in Babylon. The Sages understood "*When the LORD restored the fortunes of Zion*" as the time when the Jewish people were granted permission to return to their homeland.

The act of moving to Israel, even today, is called *aliyah*, meaning, "to ascend." Since Israel is the Holy Land, it is on a higher spiritual plane than anywhere else in the world. Going to Israel means traveling upward in the spiritual sphere. When the Jews returned to Zion from Babylon, they moved up in the world. Along the way, they recited this psalm and the other *Songs of Ascent*, leading some scholars to believe that this is how the group of psalms got their name. They were the psalms sung as the Jews ascended toward the Holy Land: "*Our mouths were filled with laughter, our tongues with songs of joy*" (v. 2).

The return to Zion was joyous, but it wasn't perfect. While many Jews joined their spiritual leader Ezra and made it to the Holy Land, most Jews chose to stay in Babylon. This was a far cry from the full restoration of Zion to her former glory. The psalmist prayed, "*Restore our fortunes, LORD, like streams in the Negev*" (v. 4). His request was for the rest of the Jewish people to join the return to Israel like streams flowing with water instead of the current trickle of drops, slowly dribbling in.

The second issue that challenged the returnees was that they lacked total sovereignty over the land. Their Jewish leader, Zerubbabel, was severely restrained by the ruling power, Persia. Full redemption meant full freedom in their land. As the psalmist didn't want to arouse the anger of the Persians, he couched his prayer in code.

Jeremiah, when describing the exile said, "*weep bitterly for him who is exiled*" (Jeremiah 22:10). Ezekiel, when describing the redemption said, "*He took one of the seedlings of the land and put it in fertile soil*" (Ezekiel 17:5). The psalmist put both ideas together and wrote, "*Those who sow with tears will reap with songs of joy*" (v. 5). He covertly prayed that just as the exile had come true as predicted, all of the redemption prophecies—including full sovereignty over Israel—should be fulfilled as well.

Today, Psalm 126 is recited before the *Grace after Meals* on the Sabbath and holidays. Every time that we are blessed with food, it's because someone sowed the seeds for our sustenance to grow. We remember that just as our festive meals are a product of hard work and labor, so, too, the exile will be a difficult experience, but one that will bear fruit. Though we still weep, sometimes bitterly, the time will come when we will reap with songs of joy.

A CHRISTIAN SONG

Bringing in the Sheaves

BASED ON PSALM 126:6)

Sowing in the morning,
*   sowing seeds of kindness,*

Sowing in the noontide
*   and the dewy eve;*

Waiting for the harvest,
*   and the time of reaping,*

We shall come rejoicing,
*   bringing in the sheaves.*

Refrain:

Bringing in the sheaves,
*   bringing in the sheaves,*

We shall come rejoicing,
*   bringing in the sheaves;*

Bringing in the sheaves,
*   bringing in the sheaves,*

We shall come rejoicing,
*   bringing in the sheaves.*

—KNOWLES SHAW
(1834–1878)

Psalm 126

WHEN THE LORD
RESTORED THE
FORTUNES OF
ZION, WE WERE
LIKE THOSE
WHO DREAMED.

—PSALM 126:1

Seventy Years of Slumber

The *Talmud* tells a story about a man named Honi, one of the most righteous men in his generation and the greatest scholar around. But one verse puzzled him his entire life: "*When the LORD restored the fortunes of Zion, we were like those who dreamed.*" Honi understood that the verse was a reference to the 70 years of exile that the Jewish people experienced in Babylon. It was as if they had been sleeping for 70 years, dreaming about Zion. Honi asked, "How is it possible for someone to sleep for 70 years?"

Now, of course, Honi understood that the Jews didn't literally sleep all those years. He understood the verse on a symbolic level. What he couldn't understand was how someone could spend virtually their entire lifetime in a spiritual slumber. Seventy years is a short time to make a difference in the world and earn life in the world to come. How could anyone waste it?

One day, Honi got his answer. Honi noticed a young man planting a carob tree by the side of the road, so he stopped to say, "Don't you know that it takes 70 years for a carob tree to bear fruit. Do you really expect to eat it?" The man explained, "When I came into the world there were carob trees with fruit that were planted by my grandfather. Just as he planted for me, I plant for my grandchildren." The story continues that Honi sat down to eat and then fell asleep for 70 years. When he woke up, he saw children eating from the carob tree that had been planted 70 years earlier.

DEVOTION

The Sages explain the story this way: In this story, Honi is the man who sleeps for 70 years and the young man is the righteous individual who uses his lifetime wisely. Honi learns that people waste their life away because they don't see a point in working on something that they won't benefit from  immediately. The reward for living a meaningful life takes many years to receive, and often, it is only received after one's lifetime.

Like the carob tree, the fruits of righteousness take a long time to grow. But the young man is like a righteous individual who spends his life working hard to make the world a better place anyway. He knows that the reward may be long in coming, but it will follow.

With all of the comforts of modern day life, many people sleep through an entire lifetime. Recreation is important, but it's not what makes a life well lived. God won't ask you how many baseball games you watched, but how much time you spent playing ball with your kids. He won't ask how many novels you read, but how much time you spent reading the Bible.

Planting seeds requires work and can be difficult at times. But that's the only way to grow trees that will bear fruit for eternity.

GOING DEEPER FOR CHRISTIANS

For a Christian perspective on bearing fruit, read:

- Matthew 3:7–9
- Luke 6:43–45
- John 15:5
- Romans 7:4
- Galatians 5:22

PSALM 128

BLESSED ARE
ALL WHO FEAR
THE LORD,
WHO WALK IN
OBEDIENCE
TO HIM.

—PSALM 128:1

A SONG FOR BLESSINGS

Psalm 128 is a beautiful description of the blessings that will come upon a person who lives in fear of the Lord. Such a person will eat the fruits of his or her labor and experience prosperity. Each will be blessed with a loving family and long life. Health, wealth, and happiness—the person who fears God is blessed with it all.

In Hebrew, the word for "fear" and the word for "see" come from the same three-letter root. In the Hebrew language, when two words are spelled alike, they are connected. In our psalm, there are two themes. The first is fearing God, "*Blessed are all who fear the LORD*" (v.1). The second is the blessings that one will see, "*May you see the prosperity of Jerusalem*" (v. 5);

"*May you live to see your children's children*" (v. 6). There is a clear connection between fearing and seeing. What we fear determines what we will see. If we fear the Lord, we will see blessings.

Tradition teaches that in Temple times, when pilgrims would ascend to Jerusalem for holidays, they would sing psalms on the way. This psalm, along with the other *Songs of Ascent*, were the psalms that they recited. With the theme of Jerusalem in all her glory, we can imagine the significance of this song as the pilgrims made their way to the holy city. They were on their way to see the very blessings described in this psalm.

Today, Psalm 128 is included whenever special prayer services are held for the State of Israel. Among the blessings mentioned in this psalm are to see Jerusalem thrive and to see peace in Israel. We continue to pray that we merit seeing the prosperity of Jerusalem and a safe Israel at peace.

Psalm 128 is also read on Saturday nights just after the Sabbath ends. In Judaism, the "day" starts at sunset. The Bible says: "*And there was evening, and there was morning—the first day*" (Genesis 1:5). This means that every day begins at sundown, the night before. It also means that when God created the world, it began on Saturday night. It's the time when nothing became something. Tradition teaches that even today Saturday night retains some of that creative energy.

With all of its blessings and goodness, Psalm 128 is most appropriate for Saturday night. As we begin the week ahead, we pray that it be filled with all good things. We tap into the energy of creativity and ask God to bring our prayers into reality. It is a time for requests, but also a time to consider our responsibilities. We remember that our job is to fear the Lord as we ask Him to provide the blessings that we would like to see in our lives.

A CHRISTIAN SONG

O Happy Man, Whose Soul Is Filled

BASED ON PSALM 128

O happy man,
    whose soul is filled

With zeal and reverent awe!

His lips to God
    their honors yield,

His life adorns the law.

A careful providence
    shall stand

And ever guard thy head,

Shall on the labors
    of thy hand

Its kindly blessings shed.

—Isaac Watts (1674–1748)

Psalm 128

MAY THE

LORD BLESS

YOU FROM

ZION; MAY

YOU SEE THE

PROSPERITY

OF JERUSALEM.

—PSALM 128:5

The Beauty of Jerusalem

Israel tourism has peaked dramatically in the last several years.
More and more people are making the spiritual journey to Jerusalem.
But not everyone sees the same thing. Psalm 128 says, "*May you see the
prosperity of Jerusalem.*" But the goodness of Jerusalem is not something
that everyone can see.

Shortly after World War II, Rabbi Kook, son of the first chief rabbi
of Israel, was sitting in Jerusalem at his Sabbath table. His students were
expressing their concern about tourists who were coming to the new country
and leaving with a bad report on their lips. "They complain about the heat, the
poverty, the backwardness, the political situation—and discourage others from
coming here!" the students said. The Rabbi responded with the following story:

*There was once a wealthy young man who wanted to marry
a certain young lady. She was the prettiest girl in town and had
a beautiful personality to match. Since the girl came from a poor
family, her parents were excited about the match. But the girl was not
interested in the boy. From what she had heard, he was shallow and
rude. She refused to even meet him. The father, who was anxious about
his daughter's finding another match as attractive, pressured the girl
into going on just one date. She reluctantly agreed.*

*The night of the date arrived, but it ended before it even began.
When the young man arrived, his date came out with her hair
uncombed, wearing a crumpled dress, and shabby slipper shoes.*

DEVOTION

The boy was appalled and quickly made excuses for why he had to leave.

"What everyone says about this girl—it's not true!" he tells his friends. "She's a hideous old hag!"

Rabbi Kook then explained his parable. While it may seem that the young fellow was rejecting the young woman, the truth is that it was she who rejected him. So, too, Jerusalem does not reveal her beauty to everyone. The *Talmud* teaches that ten portions of beauty came down into the world, nine of them to Jerusalem. But only those deserving will behold the beauty that she is.

Two people can look at the exact same thing and yet see that thing differently. What we see is just as much dependent on who we are as what we are looking at. How we see other people says little about them, but speaks volumes about us. If we are superficial and focus on physicality, then we will only see the surface of the people and the world around us. But if we are spiritual people who appreciate the godliness in everything, then we will see the world for the divine creation that it is, and we will see people for the beautiful souls that they are. When we see ugliness around us, we need to take a moment and look within ourselves. Beautify yourself on the inside and you will see beauty everywhere else. Including Jerusalem.

GOING DEEPER FOR CHRISTIANS

For a Christian perspective on spiritual sight, read:

- 1 Corinthians 13:12
- 2 Corinthians 3:18
- 2 Corinthians 5:7
- 1 John 3:2

PSALM 130

OUT OF THE
DEPTHS I CRY
TO YOU, LORD;
LORD, HEAR
MY VOICE. LET
YOUR EARS
BE ATTENTIVE
TO MY CRY
FOR MERCY.

—PSALM 130:1–2

A SONG OF CONFESSION

Psalm 130 was written from a deep place, "*Out of the depths I cry to you, LORD*" (v. 1). But where is this deep place and why does it matter?

One opinion is that King David wrote this psalm for the generations who would be living in the exile. If Jerusalem and the Holy Land are considered to be on a higher spiritual plane, then all other places in the world, including any place in exile, would be comparatively lower. David knew there would be a time when the children of Israel would find themselves struggling in a foreign land. He wrote this psalm to help them find their way back into the Promised Land.

Others feel that "*the depths*" in this psalm is a reference to a spiritual low. As David revealed in other psalms, this was certainly something he experienced. David's sin with Bathsheba is a repetitive theme in the book of Psalms. This would explain the middle of the psalm which talks about forgiveness: "*But with you there is forgiveness*" (v. 4). Though the psalmist might have felt he had reached

rock bottom, this psalm is a reassurance that there is always a way out. No matter how low we have fallen, we can always get back up again.

There is yet another understanding of this psalm that doesn't attach it to a particular time period or a specific situation. This more general perspective has made it one of the most famous psalms of all. The word "depth" is often used in the Bible to mean the depths of the sea. For example, elsewhere in psalms David writes: *"I have come into the deep waters; the floods engulf me"* (Psalm 69:2).

Psalm 130 was written for anyone who feels like they are sinking in very deep waters. Be it illness, danger, war, or any kind of challenge—financial or other—this psalm gives voice to our cry for help. When we feel that we are sinking into the depths, this psalm is a ladder out. Appropriately, Psalm 130 belongs to the *Songs of Ascent*, a fitting title for a psalm that helps people ascend out of the depths and back onto the safety of dry land.

Unofficially, Psalm 130 is one of the most-used psalms. It's the one that we turn to in times of trouble and crisis. But the psalm has a place in liturgy as well. It is said during the Ten Days of Repentance—the time between *Rosh Hashanah* and *Yom Kippur*, which is designated for intense introspection and prayer.

On *Rosh Hashanah*, God decides the fate of every person. But it isn't until *Yom Kippur* that our fate is sealed. The time between can sway our destiny one way or the other. We recite this psalm and pray that God will forgive our sins, save us from all trouble, and grant us a good new year.

A CHRISTIAN SONG

Jesus, Lover of My Soul

BASED ON PSALM 130:7

Jesus, lover of my soul,

Let me to thy bosom fly,

While the nearer waters roll,

While the tempest
still is high;

Hide me, oh,
my Savior, hide,

Till the storm
of life is past;

Safe into the haven guide,

O receive my soul at last.

—CHARLES WESLEY
(1707–1788)

Psalm 130

IF YOU, LORD,
KEPT A RECORD OF
SINS, LORD, WHO
COULD STAND?

—PSALM 130:3

Letting Go

In Psalm 130, King David makes a good case. He says: "*If you, LORD, kept a record of sins, LORD, who could stand?*" In other words, everyone in the world makes mistakes. If God were keeping track, we'd all be doomed! David says, "No one would be able to stand before You, God, if You held us accountable every time that we messed up." In order for humanity to exist, God must have mercy and be forgiving. And that's the good news: "*But with you there is forgiveness*" (v. 4).

David is right. Mercy and forgiveness are great solutions to the problem of man's fallibility. But God has a much better idea.

In the book of Ezra, we learn about a period when the children of Israel are steeped in sin. The Jews were exiled by the Babylonians, and then 70 years later, some of them returned to Israel. Ezra was one of them. When he arrived in Israel, he was saddened and shocked to find that those in the Holy Land had fallen to an unprecedented spiritual low.

He wept before God and acknowledged that "*our sins are higher than our heads and our guilt has reached to the heavens*" (Ezra 9:6). Like David in Psalm 130, he said, "*Here we are before you in our guilt, though because of it not one of us can stand in your presence*" (Ezra 9:15). Ezra begged God for mercy because he knew that the Jews were totally deserving of punishment.

DEVOTION

The Sages teach that the situation that Ezra prayed about can be compared to a man crossing a river with a large knapsack on his head. His feet begin to sink into the mud, and he realizes that he is in danger of sinking beneath the water. The people who see him call out, "Let go of your pack so that you will be able to free your feet!"

So, too, the rabbis teach, God says, "Why do you say *'If you, Lord, kept a record of sins, Lord, who could stand?'* Let he who has sinned rather repent of his wicked ways. Let him let go of his sins, and I will have mercy on him."

People often say, "I know that I should stop doing X, but I just don't know how!" If you were holding a hot potato, would you know how to drop it? I imagine so. When we recognize that something is hurting us, we are able to let it go.

Our sins are like baggage that weigh us down and hold us back. Free yourself from sin, says God, and watch how far you can go.

GOING DEEPER FOR CHRISTIANS

For a Christian perspective on confession, read:

- Matthew 3:1–6
- James 5:16
- 1 John 1:9

PSALM 133

IT IS AS IF THE
DEW OF HERMON
WERE FALLING ON
MOUNT ZION.
FOR THERE THE
LORD BESTOWS
HIS BLESSING,
EVEN LIFE
FOREVERMORE.

—PSALM 133:3

A SONG FOR THE GIFT OF RAIN

Tradition teaches that King David accidently opened up the source of all water. Although he wouldn't be the one to build God's Temple, King David was determined to build its foundation. As he dug on the Temple Mount, he unknowingly removed what had been the cover of the "waters of the deep." These waters were unlike any other body of water in the world. This was the source of all other sources! Now unleashed, the waters began to rise and threatened to flood the entire world.

Thankfully, David was able to prevent the greatest catastrophe since the times of Noah. He wrote the name of God on a shard of earthenware and threw it into the water. The waters began to subside. But when they finished

their descent, there was a new problem. The waters had receded 16 thousand cubits below the land.

David realized that with the water so deep within the earth, nothing would be able to grow. The Sages teach that he recited the 15 *Songs of Ascent*, and the waters rose 15 thousand cubits. According to some, that's how these psalms got their title. They caused the waters to ascend and bless the world once more.

Psalm 133 is the fourteenth of the 15 *Songs of Ascent*. It is a three-verse psalm about blessings that fits well with the story behind the psalm's creation. The psalmist wrote, *"It is as if the dew of Hermon were falling on Mount Zion. For there the L*ORD *bestows his blessing, even life forevermore"* (v. 3).

We can imagine David standing over the waters as they began to rise. As he saw them draw near, he described how these waters from Zion would flow to the rest of the world, like dew streaming down a mountain. Water is the symbol for all blessings because it gives life and helps everything grow. Just as the source of all water was found in Zion, all blessings would come from her as well.

This psalm is recited in the afternoon prayer service, but only between the holidays of *Sukkot* and Passover. This is because the months between the two holidays are the winter months, which in Israel, are the only time that it rains. It is during these months that God sends blessings down to earth. The rest of the year is for absorbing the rain waters which produce the flowers that we see in the spring and the fruits that we enjoy in summer and fall.

In most countries around the world, rain isn't well-received. It dims the sun and spoils outdoor activities. But in Israel, cold, wet rain is a cause for celebration. For a country that struggles with drought, everyone understands that rain is a gift. Israelis don't just call the wet stuff falling from the sky rain; they call it "rains of blessing." This psalm is a prayer for a rainy winter so that we can enjoy God's blessings all year long.

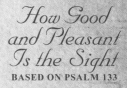

A CHRISTIAN SONG

How Good and Pleasant Is the Sight
BASED ON PSALM 133

*How good and pleasant
    is the sight*

*when Christians make
    it their delight*

to live in blest accord;

*such love is like
    anointing oil*

*that consecrates
    for holy toil*

the servants of the Lord.

—PSALTER, 1912

Psalm 133

HOW GOOD AND

PLEASANT IT IS

WHEN GOD'S

PEOPLE LIVE

TOGETHER

IN UNITY.

—PSALM 133:1

United We Stand

In the first century B.C.E., Judea was ruled by a queen known as Shlomtzion. Her name had been Alexandra, but because she brought peace to a nation fraught with violence, she became known as "she who makes peace in Zion," in Hebrew, Shlomtzion.

Shlomtzion's life was mostly full of strife. She was married to an evil monarch who imprisoned his own brothers and starved his mother, all in an attempt to hold onto his power. At the time, the Jewish people were also in the midst of a ruthless internal battle between those who favored a more secular way of living and those who adhered to the Bible and its laws.

Shlomtzion's husband became ill and eventually died. The first thing she did was set his family free. The next thing she did was marry her deceased husband's brother, the custom in Jewish law. But as it turned out, Shlomtzion's second husband was just as bad as the first. The country continued to be racked with violence and internal strife. Eventually, that husband died, and Shlomtzion became the ruler of Judea. For nine years, until her death, Judea enjoyed unprecedented peace.

As ruler, Queen Shlomtzion devoted her effort into restoring peace and harmony to her broken land. She negotiated compromises and brought the Bible back to the mainstream. The *Talmud* describes how the produce grown during that brief window of time was unnaturally abundant. Wheat grew to the size of kidney beans; oats, to the size of olives; and lentils, to the size of large coins. The blessing of abundance that was showered on the land was

DEVOTION

attributed to the accomplishments of Queen Shlomtzion. The rabbis preserved some of the produce for future generations to show them what is possible when people can live together in peace and with righteousness.

Every Friday night before the Sabbath meal begins, there is a custom for parents to bless their children. For girls, we say "May God make you like Sarah, Rebecca, Rachel, and Leah." But for boys, we say, "May God make you like Ephraim and Manasseh."

Why not Abraham, Isaac, and Jacob? The answer is, because Ephraim and Manasseh were the first brothers descended from Abraham to be at peace with each other. Isaac struggled with Ishmael, and Jacob had to contend with Esau. Jacob's children sold their brother Joseph into slavery. But Joseph's sons, Ephraim and Manasseh, loved each other and lived in unity. We bless our children that they should be like them because unity brings all other blessings into the world.

In Psalm 133 King David wrote, "*How good and pleasant it is when God's people live together in unity.*" As the brief era of Queen Shlomtzion showed us, it is beneficial for everyone to live in unity. Anytime you can make peace, and anywhere you can bring peace, make every effort to do so. As we bless each other, God will bless the world.

GOING DEEPER FOR CHRISTIANS

For a Christian perspective on unity, read:

- John 17:23
- Romans 12:5
- 1 Corinthians 12:12–13
- Ephesians 4:2-6

PSALM 137

HOW CAN WE
SING THE SONGS
OF THE LORD
WHILE IN A
FOREIGN LAND?
IF I FORGET
YOU, JERUSALEM,
MAY MY RIGHT
HAND FORGET
ITS SKILL.

—PSALM 137:4–5

A SONG OF LAMENT

"*By the rivers of Babylon we sat and wept when we remembered Zion*" (v. 1). The opening verse of Psalm 137 gives us the setting, but who are the characters in this scene? The Sages teach that this psalm was composed by the priests who had just been exiled from Israel by the Babylonians. They sat and wept in their captors' land for all that they had lost.

Then the priests did something strange. They took their musical instruments—the ones that they would have used in the Temple service—and hung them on trees. The priests were depressed because they could no longer make music in God's Temple. Their harps were now useless. But why hang the instruments? They should have destroyed them instead!

Around this time, Ezekiel, who was both a priest and a prophet, had his famous vision at the Kebar River in Babylon. He saw the chariot of God and His entourage going into exile with the Jewish people. Ezekiel explained that the vision was a reassurance that the Jews would someday return to Israel and that God was surely with them. One day, He would return with them as well. This was the only comfort that the priests had as they mourned. They hung their harps by the river—the place of Ezekiel's vision—as a reminder that one day, they would use their harps again.

In the next part of the psalm, the Babylonians watched as the priests put their harps away and encouraged them to take the instruments down. In essence, they said, "Don't be depressed! You can sing here, too!" But the priests replied, "*How can we sing the songs of the LORD while in a foreign land?*" (v. 4). It's just not the same, according to the priests. There was one land where they could fully serve God.

This leads into the famous words: "*If I forget you, Jerusalem, may my right hand forget its skill*" (v. 5). The priests realized that with time, the Jews would acclimate to their new home. They decided then and there to make it a point to remember Jerusalem during times of joy. This was to remind the Jews then, and us today, that our joy will never be complete until the Jewish people return to Zion.

Today, every Jewish wedding ceremony ends with the same words, "*If I forget you, Jerusalem. . . .*" After reciting this verse, the groom breaks a glass, representing Jerusalem's destruction. A wedding is the most joyful occasion there is, and so it is precisely then that we need to remember that Jerusalem is still not what she once was.

Psalm 137 is recited before the *Grace after Meals* at every meal, except for the meals we eat on the Sabbath and holidays. Its sad theme is not appropriate for those days. But every other day of the week, just after we have eaten and are satisfied, we remember that true satisfaction will only come when Zion is fully restored to her former glory.

A CHRISTIAN SONG

I Love Thy Kingdom, Lord

BASED ON PSALM 137:5

I love Thy kingdom, Lord,

The house of Thine abode,

The church our blest
  Redeemer saved

With His own
  precious blood.

For her my tears shall fall;

For her my prayers ascend;

To her my cares
  and toils be given,

Till toils and cares shall end.

—TIMOTHY DWIGHT
(1752–1817)

Psalm 137

BY THE RIVERS
OF BABYLON WE
SAT AND WEPT
WHEN WE
REMEMBERED
ZION.

—PSALM 137:1

The Gates of Tears

The Babylonians were very clever. When they exiled the Jews from Israel, they did not let them stop to rest on the way. They understood the power of tears. If the Jews had a moment to stop and think, surely they would have cried out to their God. The Babylonians understood that those tears could disrupt their plan. Psalm 137 describes how once the Jews got the chance to sit, they wept. But at that point it was too late. They were already *by the rivers of Babylon.*

The Sages point out that when the Jews sat and cried, they had just lost everything—their homes, their businesses, their land, and their way of life. But what did they cry about? They cried for Zion. *"We sat and wept when we remembered Zion."*

Finally, the Jews understood what the prophets had been trying to teach them for decades. They understood what Zion was and what it meant to them. They realized that the Jews without Zion were aimless and vulnerable, physically and spiritually. They would build new homes, find new jobs, and become acclimated to their new land. But Zion was irreplaceable.

The prophet Jeremiah saw the Jews crying and said, "Had you cried but one tear while you were still in Jerusalem, you would have never been exiled." The tears of the Jews had the power to prevent the exile, but they came too late. However, now they would have the power to bring the exile to an end.

DEVOTION

The Sages teach that there are many gates to heaven, but only one is never closed: the Gate of Tears. When someone prays to God with tears, the prayers fly straight to heaven through the Gate of Tears. But if the gate is always open, then why does it need a gate at all?

The Sages answer because not all tears are real tears. The gate is there to keep the fake tears out. We've all heard of the term "crocodile tears." Not all tears are genuine and heartfelt. Many tears are shed for no good reason at all. The tears that have the power to move heaven and earth are the kind that the Jews shed as they sat in Babylon. They were tears of genuine longing and sadness for what was truly good and now lost.

What do you cry about? Tears are not just an emotional release; they are a barometer of the soul. What we cry about tells us what we value. We only weep for the things that we truly love. The Sages teach that tears have the power to unlock all the doors that stand before us. But that's only if our tears are real.

GOING DEEPER FOR CHRISTIANS

For a Christian perspective on true remorse and sorrow, read:

- Matthew 27:3–5
- 2 Corinthians 7:8–10

PSALM 145

GREAT IS THE
LORD AND MOST
WORTHY OF PRAISE;
HIS GREATNESS NO
ONE CAN FATHOM.

—PSALM 145:3

A SONG OF CREATION

Psalm 145 is the beginning of the end. It is the first of the last six psalms in the Psalter. As a group, they are called The Conclusion of the Praise. They finish King David's epic work by stressing his goal in writing it—to praise God and inspire others to do the same.

The introduction to Psalm 145 tells us that it was composed by David and is "*A Psalm of praise,*" in Hebrew, *tehilla*. It is the only psalm given that title and is also the source of the Hebrew word for Psalms, *Tehillim*. This psalm, more than any other, represents the entire book of Psalms. It is the paramount psalm of praise.

Not surprisingly, Psalm 145 is a favorite among the Sages. They teach that anyone who recites it three times a day is guaranteed a place in heaven. What is it about this psalm that makes it so special?

Two features make Psalm 145 different from the rest. First, it is written with an acrostic structure. Each verse starts with the corresponding letter in the alphabet in order to signify that we are praising God from A to Z. The psalm is all-encompassing, using every facet of the alphabet. We get a sense of God's greatness and His mastery over the world through its words and organization.

The second prominent feature of this psalm is the verse that states, "*You open your hand and satisfy the desires of every living thing*" (v. 16). The idea that God provides for every living creature is a fundamental of faith and sums up so much of our praise. In one succinct line, David captures the essence of God's benevolence.

Psalm 145 is a super-powered psalm with a super dose of praise. But if you look closely, something is missing. Every letter in the Hebrew alphabet is represented except one—the letter "nun." While many opinions exist as to why David omitted it, the fact that he left it out is most telling. Even the greatest psalm of praise is incomplete, and its message is clear: While we can spend the rest of our lives praising God, we will never come close to describing His greatness. God is beyond description and greater than our wildest imaginations.

The Sages' advice—to say Psalm 145 three times a day—is reflected in the liturgy. It is recited twice in the morning service and once in the afternoon. However, the Sages made a slight change and added several verses. The change makes the first words of the prayer the same as the first words of the book of Psalms: "*Blessed be the one.*" It also makes the last words of the prayer the same as the last words in Psalms: "*Praise the Lord.*" This was done intentionally in order to emphasize that the prayer reflects all 150 psalms, compressed into one. These first and last words also sum up the entire book of Psalms: Blessed be the one who praises the Lord!

A CHRISTIAN SONG

All Creatures of Our God and King

BASED ON PSALM 145:10

*All creatures of
  our God and King,*

*Lift up your voice
  and with us sing,*

Alleluia, Alleluia

*Thou burning sun
  with golden beam,*

*Thou silver moon
  with softer gleam,*

*O praise Him,
  O praise Him,*

Alleluia, Alleluia, Alleluia!

—St. Francis of Assisi
(1182–1226)

Psalm 145

YOU OPEN

YOUR HAND

AND SATISFY

THE DESIRES

OF EVERY

LIVING THING

—PSALM 145:16

GOING DEEPER
FOR CHRISTIANS

For a Christian perspective
on caring for the poor, read:

- Matthew 25:31–40

- 2 Corinthians 9:8–10

- James 2:14–16

- 1 John 3:16–17

Partners in Perfection

Sometimes we wonder if we will have enough money to provide for our families. More often than not, our worries are unnecessary. Some way, somehow, we get what we need. Sometimes it's obvious, and other times it's hidden, but God is always working His miracles. As the psalmist wrote, "*You open your hand and satisfy the desires of every living thing*" (v. 16).

The Sages don't deny that there are people who are starving. But they maintain that God provides enough. They interpret our verse this way: "*You [God] open your hand*" and provide the world with plenty. But it is our job to take the sustenance from God's hand and "*satisfy the desires of every living thing.*"

There is more than enough food for everyone. We live in a world with plenty to go around. But God wants us to be His partners and make sure that the food gets where it needs to go.

Meet Clara. She died at the age of 100 and was known affectionately as Jerusalem's chicken lady. About 30 years earlier, Clara noticed a young girl collecting scraps from the butcher. The butcher explained that the girl's family had come on hard times and the scraps were their only sustenance. Clara immediately told the butcher to give the girl two chickens and a pound of chopped meat every week and charge it to her account. As Clara told others about the needy in Jerusalem, the funds trickled in. Decades later, she was responsible for feeding well over 100 families a week. From one small act came many well-fed children.

There are one billion people who are starving, but six billion of us who aren't. Imagine the difference we could make if even just a fraction of us would do our part. God does His part and provides for everyone. It's time that we do ours.